THE PILLARS
FOR SUSTAINING
LIFE

Discover What You Need
To Live An Intentional Life

DR. SAMUEL ODEKE, DSL

The Pillars For Sustaining Life: *Discover What You Need To Live an Intentional Life*
Copyright © 2018 by Dr. Samuel Odeke

ISBN 978-978-56337-9-5

Unless otherwise indicated, Scripture quotations are taken from:
The Holy Bible, New International Version (NIV). Copyright © 1973, 1978, 1984, 2011 by Biblica, Inc. ™. Used by permission. All rights reserved.
The New King James Version (NKJV). Copyright © 2013 by Holman Bible Publishers. Used by permission. All rights reserved.

Online versions used:
King James Version
Living Bible (TLB)
The Message (MSG)
New Living Translation (NLT)
Amplified Bible (AMP)

Designed by Diomerito Company, Lagos, Nigeria.
Published in Nigeria by *Media DNA*
Published in the United States by *Thebookpatch* and *Amazon Createspace*

CONTENTS

ACKNOWLEDGMENT

The work that produced this book comes from continuous learning and seeking knowledge from parents, family, friends, elders, teachers, mentors, advisors, church leaders, and counsellors among others. All these people have significantly taught me something that has impacted my life. I am humbled and eternally grateful for your contribution to my life.

Nobody can claim to accomplish something significant without external help from others. So many people have helped me pursue the dreams of sharing the ideas, insights and resources. I believe with all my heart that my purpose is to equip and empower aspiring leaders through resources, training, coaching and mentoring to serve humanity. Moreover, to achieve that purpose, I shall endeavor to live according to my virtues and values given below:

- Integrity, honesty and accountability
- Continuous learning and personal development
- Self-discipline, respect, and humility.
- Service and hard work

Honestly, we are the sum total of what we have learned from others, and we must owe any measure of success and progress to their contribution in life.

Here are a few people among many who have made this work turn out as a resource for use for

To my spouse and children, thanks for your support.

To Dr Jason Newcomb, my friend, a talented and gifted editor. Your spirit of attention to detail and excellence is impressive. Thank you for your patience and feedback on my writing skills and accepting to teach me to continue to improve my skills. You are a tremendous source of motivation and encouragement.

To members of CTSL Uganda and BCHS, you have allowed me to privilege to share and test my ideas and principles in this work through our engagements and relationships. Without you, my dreams, ideas and vision would have remained dormant.

To my friends in Lagos, Nigeria; Ayo Oshewolo and Samuel Adeyemi, thank you for your contribution to the vision and dream. You will forever be part of my history. Thank you.

DEDICATION

To the people in the world who are struggling to understand the essential things in life. May you all get the revelation in your hearts to discover these fundamental principles,

To my great mentors who have always inspired me and impacted my own life to pursue the vision for my life.

To my faithful and committed friends and family. Your trust in me and my dreams over the years continues to influence my decisions, and it is a source of my encouragement, inspiration and motivation.

To the friends and leaders who support the work of CTSL Uganda. Thanks for standing with our vision.

To the millions of people in any part of the world who are desperate to change their lives and attain a better life.

To my spouse and children. Thank you for you being the gift from God.

To the Source of All Ideas, Wisdom, Knowledge, Life, Power, Authority, Wealth, Success, Prosperity, Leadership, Vision and Sustainer of the Universe.

FOREWORD

I met Samuel on May 6, 2017, at our doctoral graduation ceremony at Regent University. God arranged our seats so we would sit beside one another. We visited briefly and later shared a meal together and with classmates and our professors. When you meet Samuel, you will notice his infectious smile and personality. You will notice his humble character. You will notice his drive and passion for helping others.

Since graduation, Samuel and I have primarily communicated through email and Skype text messages. We have developed a friendship. In Samuel, I know I have a friend who will pray for my family and me; Samuel knows he has the same with me.

When you read Samuel's work, you will experience his love for others, his humility, his character, and his passion for helping others reach their potential. Samuel is consistent in his teaching principles. He does not waver. He wants that same, unwavering foundation for you, the reader, as well.

I love options. If I had a chosen job title, it would be "options giver."

Dear reader, Samuel will give you options that have worked in his own life as well as in the lives of others. He will provide you with practical advice for creating a better life. He covers faith, family, and relationships; he covers health and wealth; he covers ideas, goal-setting, and growth among other topics. Samuel believes inside all of us are seeds of potential. He does his best with this work to help cultivate, nurture, and help those seeds grow. He truly wants you to be your best version of yourself.

Samuel wants you to reach your potential. In this work, he gives you foundational principles (or pillars) on which you can build your best life yet.

May God bless Samuel and his continued work and may God bless you, the reader.

Dr. Jason Newcomb, LCPC
Counselor
Regent University '17
September 28, 2018

PROLOGUE

Everyone you meet is fighting a battle
you know nothing about. Be kind always.
— Anonymous

The Most Important Things In Life

What would you list as the most important thing in life based the fact that living on Earth is hard? Life has so many interpretations. Some people say, "Life is a journey." Others say, "Life is tough or hard." Others think, "Life is a mystery, game, play or destination" among others. It is laborious, complicated and onerous for everyone. What makes life hard? There are diverse causes of life's hardships such as crises, problems, challenges, wars, natural disasters and human-made conflicts. Life also becomes hard when people fail. When people die, families experience difficulties or painful moments. When business collapses, the experience of loss or hopelessness sets in. When friends become enemies or critiques, you will feel hopeless. For some people, life becomes a horrible experience. When individuals or leaders lose their power, wealth, health or riches, sometimes life becomes meaningless or empty.

Have you ever seen a note left behind when someone commits suicide? Usually, the police might find a message stating, "I had no reason to live anymore." Alternatively, the message could be, "My life has been worthless or hopeless, so it is better to die." I know a friend who killed himself because of a mistake that he could not take or wanted his friends like me to know about. However, the truth that everyone makes mistakes; everyone fails; everyone does not achieve everything. Everyone has some regrets or disappointments in life. Everyone experiences pain or loss of some sort at some point in his or her lifetime. Every person wants to succeed in something. They want to be dominant and powerful. They wish to have the best in life. They want more wealth, power, riches, resources, greatness and opportunities. They want to own property, buildings, schools, hospitals and many more, including travelling to dream places. Everyone wants fame, popularity, success, wealth, happiness and good life. I have never heard a person who said, "I plan to fail." Everyone is always preparing for success or something.

However, there is pure greatness and success. I have come to understand two types: primary success and secondary success. I posted about primary and secondary greatness on my Facebook page for my friends and followers. After I had posted this information, I thought about it and decided that it was relevant to this book. I decided that you also need to read it. Here is what I thought about primary and secondary greatness or having a successful life on Earth.

Whenever I look at the way society measures greatness, I see people as the secondary type. The secondary form is achieved from dubious ways, seeking for popularity or fame. For instance, if someone has good looks, talent, or communication abilities, then he or she becomes successful in ways that do not reflect good morals and standards. Society will celebrate faster. However, the primary form of greatness and success comes from character, integrity, hard work, self-sacrifice, justice, fairness and ethics. It is built through servanthood or serving others. Humility, justice, fairness, self-discipline, self-control, good morals, hard work, and a positive attitude produce the primary form of greatness.

Meanwhile, secondary greatness is derived from manipulation, cheating and dubious ways. Secondary greatness can't last for long and evaporates like vapor. Primary greatness is long-term and built through the strengthening of character and ethics over an extended period while also overcoming all temptations against evil acts. In the end, Character is a decisive factor that matters in life when every is evaluated about a person's life. The life of a person is judged and evaluated based on their character. There are so many things that easy to do. For instance, cheating is an easy thing to do. Manipulation is also not hard. Those around you will know if you are doing what is right or wrong. They will tell if the parent, sister, brother, follower or leader is cheating. They will see. It will get exposed. So, my question what kind of greatness do you want in life? Which one are you chasing?

Now, with everything that happens in the world, what are the core things that matter in life? Someone told me that money is everything. A friend of mine told me, "You do not know the power of money." I reflected on that statement before asking some more questions.

- If you want success, how do you get it?
- If you're going to influence others, then how do you become influential?
- What are the things that make life bearable or sustainable?

My conclusion is that everything that exists or manufactured (for instance, phones, cars, desks, computers, homes, roads and so forth) is essential for survival. All these things are necessary for life, but what are the most important or essential things in life? Helen Keller said, "The best and most beautiful things in the world cannot be seen or even touched – they must be felt with the heart."1 This book is a result of seeking to put together the best and most essential things in life that are necessary for sustaining life. Those things that not seen or untouchable are what I have baptized as "Pillars of Sustaining Life." I would like you to think through these carefully. You can agree or disagree with me, but the book in your hands has been thoroughly presented on the core elements for living on Earth.

---

1   https://www.brainyquote.com/quotes/helen_keller_101301.

INTRODUCTION

Knowing yourself is the beginning of all wisdom.
— Aristotle

The Power Of Books

When I thought about writing my first book in 2015, I remembered how God gave Moses the Ten Commandments from Mount Sinai. Moses wrote the commandments down and taught them to the Israelites. The Israelites had been slaves for over 430 years. Pharaoh and Egyptians dominated them. Sometimes, I wonder how the world would have been without the 10 Commandments. Most of the nations and families took the 10 Commandments to govern and guide their families. The laws ensure order, stability and prosperity. Suppose Moses had not written them, then millions of people and several countries would have missed the most critical element needed for effectiveness and productivity. Can you imagine a nation without laws? Can you imagine a family not guided by laws? Can you imagine an institution, organization or company without policies? The simple act of Moses writing down the Ten Commandments means that he was a teacher and a leader. He taught the Israelites what he got from God. Without Moses' writing of the Ten Commandments, how would humanity know what God said?

Based on my experience with books, it is easy to destroy a physical book. However, I have learned that it is not easy to destroy the knowledge one learns from a book. I think of a book as a teacher, transferring what he or she knows to the reader. The teacher's job is to transfer their knowledge to the students or learners through teaching or course materials. When the students study the books related to the subjects or topics and review course materials, they will have an idea of what the teacher knows. When a book is made available to the students or readers, there is a conversation between them. When you pick a book from the bookstore and read it, then you interact with the author. You may never meet the author in your life, but his or her ideas will be available for you inside the book. The thoughts, ideas, and opinions of every author are always available through their works if they put them in a book, journal, magazine or any other presentation.

I have also observed when some people pick a book and read it, they begin to think differently. I recall one of my books, Overcoming Crises: Strategies for Addressing, Managing and Recovering from Any Crisis, was chosen by some Kenyan lady whom I never even met and lives in the United States of America. I remember reading a message on WhatsApp social media platform where she said, "Your book helped me." At that point, I said, "I am a mentor and a coach." What does this mean? If you read a book, it will be like having a daily, weekly or monthly interactions or conversations with the author.

One of the things I have loved about writing is that knowledge from books cannot be destroyed. Books contain ideas or the thoughts of other people. Ideas are the most powerful force on Earth, because everything that exists today was first an idea in the mind of an individual. Books also store knowledge and wisdom. How can you destroy knowledge or ideas? One day, I remember reading the book of an American author whom I never met in my life and I saw an online article that reported author's death which occurred April 2018. I never got to meet the author physically, but I had three of his books in my personal library. I looked at one book, and I said to myself, "The author is dead, but his knowledge, ideas, and work will live forever for generations and I too will die, leaving those ideas and concepts behind. Is this not a fantastic experience? You are dead, but your books are available for others to learn from you? One goal for everyone is to do something that leaves an eternal mark when you are no longer on Earth.

The passion for writing is now unstoppable. When I was growing up I used to think about my destiny and my future. You might not understand this but if you grew up as an orphan, encountered tragedies and lost loved ones, you know what I mean. You will realize that you are vulnerable all though and sometimes, you are hopeless and defenseless. For most orphans, you live in poverty, slums and horrible lifestyle.

As a result, I started to ask questions about the meaning of life. Here are the questions that guide me:

- Who am I?
- Where are my going in life?
- What can I do?
- Where did I come from?
- Why do I exist on Earth?

The answers to those questions, kept directing my decisions. Further, I discovered later as an adult that every human being is searching for something in life. Humans have inherent desires to do something with their lives. During discipleship classes, I was taught about Gifts of Holy Spirit and many other concepts. When I accepted Jesus as my savior, I also received seven gifts of the Holy Spirit included *"Wisdom, Understanding, Counsel, Fortitude, Knowledge, Piety, and the Fear of God."*[2] In the process, I examined those gifts and I discovered God's gifts to me are writing, teaching, and inspiring people among others. Those gifts are derived from the main gifts. To confirm those gifts, when I was at the Makerere University, I studied a Post Graduate course in Education. During, my teaching practice, my students liked my teaching approach.

Later, I realized during my workshops and seminars, that teaching was something that I actually enjoyed. I concluded that teaching was one gift. To confirm my gifts, I often received feedback from friends and workmates about how good I was during a presentation or teaching experience. When I started to write or post work on Social media, I could get feedback that I should write. One of my friends, Mr. Kevin Brougher from Arizona in USA, said, *"Good words, brother! God has given you a gift for thoughts and writing."* He shared this with me after purchasing one of my books. What does this mean? To me, it says I can add value and can give something that changes people's lives. It is more rewarding to know that your ideas helped someone and made them have a different perspective. The main reason why I will continue to write is that it will help someone somewhere and someday through my ideas, thoughts and knowledge.

---

2   1 Corinthians 12.

If I were to meet with the person or individuals that read my books, I would love to share about my passion for leadership development, success, questions of life, potential, purpose, planning and achieving one's vision. My heart cries when I meet people who have no idea about their mission on Earth. I am saddened when people have potential but are poor and struggling with life. I am distressed when people allow crises to destroy them instead of overcoming them. I am displeased when knowledge and ideas are all over, but people are ignorant. God's word says, "My people are perishing because of a lack of knowledge and having no vision." My goal is to share something I have learned to enable people to grow. I have never given up on reading and learning. It has been said, "To be a leader, you must be a reader." Leaders are readers. If you want to lead others, then you must be a reader all through your life. That also means you become a lifelong learner.

When I think of the best way to summarize what my books are all about, I merely teach principles that help change people's lives. Principles are universal, and they apply everywhere, at any time and in all places. I discovered that principles and laws have no respect for human views, opinions or experiences. As I continue to write, I realize my knowledge and ideas get upgraded. I have also learned that some of my ideas or thoughts come to me when I run on a treadmill or when I exercise or work out. When I get the ideas, I quickly run to write them down on my computer or in a journal. Later, I transfer and review them. Other times, I get my ideas when I am asleep or resting, then I get up to write in my journal next to my bed.

If there is one thing that has helped me is practice. If you do not practice something, you will not use it. Practice gives you an opportunity to improve. When you improve, you grow and change. I have also concluded to grow you must change. Change is the one thing that is guaranteed in life. Everything will change and nothing will stay the same forever. Let me quickly list the things that will change in your lifetime:

- Your body will change.
- Your health will change.
- Your spouse will change.
- Your children will change.
- Your siblings will change.
- Your priorities will change.
- Your career will change.
- Your interests will change.
- Your job will change.
- Your income will change.
- Your friends will change.
- Your knowledge will change.
- Your skills will change.
- Your experiences will change.
- Your environment will change.
- Your associations will change.
- Your standard of living will change.
- Your resources will change.

Things That Never Change On Earth

I think we can agree that what I have listed above are some of the things that will change. Do you agree or not? If you are honest, then you will agree with me entirely that those things will change. However, there are things that you cannot touch or change. It is impossible. What are those things that never change?

- God will not change. God does not change. God is the same, yesterday, today and forever.
- God's commandments never change.
- God's promises never to change.
- God's purposes never change.
- God's laws never change.
- God's decrees never change.
- God's ways never change.
- God's thoughts never change.
- God's precepts never change.
- God's word never changes.
- Gods plans never change.
- Gods values never change.
- God's principles never change.

The Key Points to Remember:

- Become a reader, so you will become a leader.
- Learn all the secrets, laws, principles and values.
- Laws are the foundation of everything.
- Laws contain in them consequences or prizes.

Chapter 1

BECOMING A CHAMPION OF DESTINY

Once you stop learning, you start dying.
*— **Albert Einstein***

A Champion Is The Greatest, Top-Notch Person

Are you becoming a champion of your destiny? How can you describe your life? Are you achieving what you desire? Are you accomplishing important things, as you should be? How does your prospect look like for the future? How do you spend your time? Some people complain while others do not. I have interacted with different people from all continents. Humans are the same everywhere in the world with similar needs, desires, hopes and aspirations. Each person has 24 hours in a day. Nobody has more time than anyone else.

However, I have observed that some are happy whereas others are miserable. Some are successful while others are unsuccessful. Some are poor and others rich. Why? What is the secret? Where is the advantage? I believe it lies in today's efforts. The secret of your successful journey is a product of your daily agenda, actions and emotions. If you can learn to have positive feelings and attitudes and make critical decisions to manage your schedule, emotions/attitudes and actions, then you will accomplish more. The rate of acceleration towards success and goals will be faster and you will succeed. The reverse is also true. The capacity to handle emotions and attitudes determines one's success rate.

Impact of Bad Feelings

Have you imagined the effects of bad attitudes on goals? What does a bad attitude do to you? Slows you down, right? Become aware that every negative thought brings negative attitudes and negates action. I have discovered that it rains on the rich and the poor at the same time. They receive the same amount of rain. The difference is the rich get up. They don't complain that it rained on me. However, the poor, who are the majority, complains it rained too much today. I'm going to let you in on a secret: You will never change your life by complaining or blaming the rain, weather, situations, circumstances, family, friends etc. The only way for you to change something is by making a personal choice to change. Nobody will make that choice and decision except YOU. You must change how and what you do daily. First stop, however, the habits of blaming or complaining. You should stop saying, "It is raining; "It is too hot;" "Life is hard;" or "The road is blocked" among other complaints people make. These are petty issues. I believe every person must own up and take personal responsibility for their lives, choices and decisions.

Success does not suddenly occur one day. It is someone's daily plan of action that determines his or her success. Success or failure is a process, not an event that suddenly occurs. Every day we either prepare for success or prepare for failure. Our lives are a result of what we do every day. What are you doing? What did you today? Did you go to the office? Did you call your partners? Did you read a book? Did you exercise in the gym? Did you do your report? Did you talk to your spouse? Did you complain? Did you blame someone? Did you meditate? Did you pray? Did you do something that is taking your closer to your dreams or goals? Did you train? Did you practice? Did you review your goals? Did you encourage someone? Did you inspire someone? What did you do that produced positive results?

Life Is Simple Only If You Have a Clear Purpose

Life is both simple and complex. The way you live your life today is a preparation for your life tomorrow or next week, next months or 10 years from today. What are you doing with your life? What are you doing with your time? Are you preparing to win or lose? Are you getting ready for success or failure? If you do not change, you will pay or play. You can decide to pay now or play later or play now and pay later. Either way, you will be asked by the universe to pay. The point is you can take it easy now and then see later or do what is required today. If you don't, your life will be harder later.

However, if you work hard now, miracles may happen to you that make you grow, learn and reap. You will reap what you sow. Remember, you only harvest after sowing. It is a law of nature. If you ever understand the laws of the universe, then life becomes simple. Natural laws cannot be ignored or violated. Another point I want to make is this: "You must be willing to do the things other people don't want to do today in order to have things others won't have tomorrow."

"You must be willing to do the things other people don't want to do today in order to have things others won't have tomorrow."

The Law of Preparation

There is an ancient story of an old ant and grasshopper. During the summer and the fall, the ant continually kept on working to gather food as the grasshopper was playing all summer. The grasshopper enjoyed his life in the summer. When the cold of the winter finally set in, the ant retired to his home and started to enjoy life. The ant paid the price for leisure but then grasshopper's time to pay came later. Guess what happens to a grasshopper. He starves in the cold because he has been preparing to fail, not for success If you prepare for tomorrow by doing something valuable today, you might not pay but play. Is it easy? It is rough, tedious and laborious.

However, everything valuable in life has a price that must be paid. There are free things in life, which are gifted by nature, but valuable things come with a price. Payment can be now or later. If you are a youth or middle-aged person, if you play during the spring season, you might pay in the summer or fall. Life is as simple as that in the sense that, you choose to pay or play. That choice is in your hands every day. Rory Vaden in his book; Take the Stairs says, "Short-term pain; long-term gain."

Yesterday, Today and Tomorrow

How do we create success and avoid failure? This is an interesting question. There are many things that I can write about this. In fact, I can write several pages, but I will focus on time: Yesterday, today and tomorrow. What will you do with these three? Allow me to highlight a couple of points:

1. Focus On Today

The only time you own is today. Do not waste your time. Do what you are expected to do. Do all you can and leave what you are unable for the next day. If you have things that are impossible and defy your intelligence, leave them to God. You cannot do everything. Today is the only time that you have, and yet most people let the day pass by or slip through their fingers. Have you ever heard people say, "We passing or killing time"? What thoughts come to your mind when you hear such statements? I think the person is saying, "I am throwing my life away," or "I am killing myself." I think about time every other minute. So many things run in my mind. Benjamin Franklin noted, "Time is the stuff life is made of." I also recall Benjamin Franklin saying, "Time is money." Can you think of those statements? Whatever you do now is what will determine the results for your life. They will influence your vision, dreams, passions, and legacy.

2. Never Focus On Yesterday

The truth is that yesterday is history. If you failed to do what you had planned, then you missed it. If you had decided to read two chapters of a book, then you lost that opportunity. You cannot bring back yesterday. You cannot change yesterday to today. The past and present results of life are related to the events of yesterday. What you did in the past is manifested in the achievements, successes, and failures. The only benefits of yesterday are the lessons you derive from it. You might have encountered obstacles, setbacks, challenges, problems, and rejection that happens to all humanity. No human being is immune to tests or problems. These adverse events or life experiences often shape us and mold us.

In my case, the negative experiences and setbacks have served to be my motivation and inspiration to do more than others. I am motivated by the fact that I can achieve anything. My beliefs are stronger than tests or problems. The danger with negative experiences is they keep reoccurring, emerging and appearing through our thoughts and attitudes. To overcome them, you need to renew your mind and avoid talking about those situations continually. If people who hurt you caused those situations, then avoid those people. Never expose yourself to the associations of the people that might have contributed to the negative experiences. Your exposure often causes you to relive and remember what happened at the time. One more thing about yesterday: It ended last night at midnight. You can start again today to strive to reach your goals. Clear goals make their achievement faster than vague ones.

3.   Do not be concerned about tomorrow

How do you see tomorrow? What is your perception? All you can do about tomorrow is to plan for what you want to do. You need a vision of the future. You need strong faith. Otherwise, you will live by sight. Living by sight is depressing. As a person who wants to succeed, you must live life according to vision or faith. Otherwise, without vision, you perish. Whatever you encounter on each day can destroy you. My book on *Strategic Planning: Understanding the 3 P's—The Power, Purpose and Process*, outlines questions you need to answer first. In addition to those questions, here are a few more:

- Do you expect your annual income to go up or down?
- Do you expect to achieve your goals, yes or no?
- Do you expect to succeed or fail?
- Do you expect your network to increase or decrease?

- Do you expect more or fewer opportunities?
- Do you expect your relationships to be strong or weak?
- Do you expect wonderful friendships or not?
- Do you plan to have stronger or weaker faith?
- Do you expect growth or not?
- Do you expect better health or not?

Preparation Is the Key to The Success Zone

Preparation is the process of getting ready for something. There are many things in life in which, when performed without preparation, you expect disaster or failure. Here are some things for which we need to prepare:

- We prepare for college.
- We prepare for marriage.
- We prepare for the holidays.
- We prepare for a vocation.
- We prepare to sleep.
- We prepare for a date.
- We prepare for war or battle.
- We prepare for opportunities.
- We prepare for a meeting.
- We prepare for work.
- We prepare to go to church.
- We prepare for interviews.

Why Is Preparation Critical?

Have you imagined an athlete going for a Boston or London marathon without preparation? What result does such an athlete expect? Have you imagined soldiers going to war without preparation? What do you expect? The answer is simple: defeat and humiliation. Before I offer the significance of preparation, I want to advise that you must prepare always. The following are reason for preparation:

- **Preparation gives you the confidence to win:** If you want to win tomorrow, then you must prepare today. What you do today will prepare you for tomorrow and in the future. If you waste your day, then your future has no guarantees. Your degree of confidence is related to the level of your preparation. Do you remember when you walked into an examination room in high school, and all you thought was "I will pass my exams"? You felt confident because you prepared thoroughly. You can apply the same concept to your life. When you are prepared, you will have nothing to fear. If you want to overcome life's challenges, then you must develop a habit of preparing. Each day of your life must be a preparation for the next one, it is like putting money into your savings bank account. A person who prepares overcomes the challenges that come with life.

- **Preparation enables you to succeed:** Most people are passive about life. They are casual about life. They think life is simple, but, life is a serious thing or business. If you have never suffered any loss or crises, then you might not understand what I am talking about here. Life requires that you prepare and be proactive. Life does not favor those who are reactive. To be effective, you must stop being a reactive person. Instead, aspire to be a proactive person. Some people think they are favored or blessed; I do not know to what extent. However, nobody gets a second chance to relive yesterday. You only have today, and for that matter, you must be proactive. A person who is proactive always focuses on preparing while a person who is reactive focuses on repairing.

- **Preparing is a great thing to do:** It allows you to have control and focus on your day. It increases your efficiency and effectiveness. It gives and increases your confidence. It saves you from losing money and time. It pays now for tomorrow. It also takes you up in life or higher level.

- **Repairing is never a good thing to do:** Repairing always focuses on the past (like yesterday) and wastes time. It also causes discouragement, results in increased costs, lost opportunities, and always makes growth slow. Avoid the idea of repairing. Focus on preparing. Preparing will often lead to success. It makes you win. The 19th Century British Prime Minister, Benjamin Disraeli, said, "The secret of success is to be ready when your opportunity comes."[3] When you are ready for success, then you can become successful.

What Are You Preparing for Today?

To have an impact, everyone must entirely focus on today. There are many horrible and tragic experiences where people lost opportunities, lives and lived miserable lives because of their failure to focus on today. There is always too much at stake if today is not effectively utilized. I believe that everyone has the choice, power and capacity to impact their lives or decide what happens. It is never too late. There is only one way to do this: Focus on today. Benjamin Franklin said, "Without continual growth and progress, such words as improvement, achievement, and success have no meaning."[4] This is important. Furthermore, Benjamin Franklin said, "One today is worth two tomorrows: What I am to be, I am now becoming."[5] That makes sense to me because what you do today is what you will become tomorrow. What you did five or ten years ago is what you have become now.

---

3   https://www.brainyquote.com/quotes/benjamin_disraeli_129996.

4   https://due.com/blog/benjamin-franklin-growth-and-progress/.

5   https://www.brainyquote.com/quotes/benjamin_franklin_151646.

Today Is Yours; It Is in Your Hands

Whenever I think about my end on Earth, it makes me wake up and work even harder. Most people never mind about their lives, legacy and purpose. How you live your life is a result of how you have prepared or not prepared in the past. Some people have no idea that yesterday is gone, and tomorrow is not guaranteed for them. Yet, still they waste today. I believe today is the only day that you have and possess. If you waste today, then you are wasting your life. To change your life, you must decide to change what you do with your "today." There will be no change in your life until you make the choice and decision to change some things that you do daily.

There will be no change in your life until you make the choice and decision to change some things that you do daily.

I believe there are somethings that you are doing that are not beneficial to you; instead, they are destructive. For instance, you spend your time listening to music from 6-9 PM or drinking alcohol from a bar or pub from 6-11PM or anything you think is beneficial. Do you realize that success does not just happen? It is a result of what is done daily. The same is true even for failure. Success is a process, not an event. Failure is also a process, not an event. I believe every day in a person's life is a preparation for the next day that you have not yet lived. Therefore, what you become in life is a result of what you do every day.

Misconceptions About Success: What People Accept as Truth

1. Most people have believed that success is almost impossible, so they give up. M. Scott Peck, MD, the writer and author of *The Road Less Travelled*, started the book with the statement, "Life is difficult."[6] He further says, "Most do not fully see this truth that life is difficult. Instead, they moan incessantly... about the enormity of their problems, their burdens, and their difficulties as if life were generally easy as if it should be easy."[7] If you think this way, you are going to be caught up in many challenges. However, I believe that if you give up, then success becomes impossible. If you do things that are easy, life will be hard for you. However, if you work hard on yourself, then life will be easy for you. When people fail, then they quit. I heard a statement that has stayed with me about winning and quitting: "Winners never quit, and quitters never win." Is this true? Most people who knew me from childhood know I never give up. They think I am successful, and yes, I am. Why? It's because I never quit. By the time I quit, it means I have tried my level best and then I let go.

2. Most people think success is about acquiring things. What is a success? How do you measure success? To me, success is not about the accumulation of things, assets, money or power. It is about doing something you are created to do. Some people think that being employed is some form of success, but in reality it is not. Employment might give you some form of comfort because you receive some income and benefits, rewards and privileges. These things never give you success. Success is your capacity to achieve your goals or doing the things you were created to accomplish. For

6   M.Scott Peck, *The Road Less Travelled* (New York: Touchstone, 1978), 15.

7   Ibid,15.

instance, how do you know a car is successful? The answer is when it performs its intended purpose effectively for its creation. When a car performs its intended or original purpose, then it is successful otherwise it is the car is a failure. How do you know the smartphone is successful? The same principle applies just as it does to humans. If you do what you are created to do, then you are successful. Success is performance of the original reason for creation.

3. Most people believe that success is for a chosen few. There are those who think they are unlucky. They believe they are cursed. They believe God is against them. However, the truth is God is against nobody. God loves everyone. God hates the sin but loves us. So, when we repent, God forgives us. Repenting is turning away from sin. God is the manufacturer; He desires everyone to be successful and prosperous. God instructed Joshua to obey His commandments. In fact, it says, "Only be strong and very courageous, that you may observe to do according to all the law which Moses My servant commanded you; do not turn from it to the right hand or to the left, that you may prosper wherever you go."[8]

Now, I want you to imagine Toyota making some cars. Do they plan for some of their products to be successful and perform effectively while others are wasted? Is this possible? Apparently, no; the Toyota Corporation wants all their products to be successful and perform to the best of their ability or potential.

4. Most people search for success or strive to be successful. Is this the case with you? Success is a simple thing: doing what you are created to do. If you do and follow all instructions of the manufacturer of your car, smartphone, and refrigerator, it will function for you.

---

8   Joshua 1:7.

If you obey God, you will succeed and prosper. What do you obey? You obey his words, commandments, laws, decrees, and statutes. You follow His ways and precepts. You do not need any revelation or anointing; all you need is to obey. Obedience to the laws of God is the key to success. If you obey the instructions in a manual that comes with a smartphone, then success is automatic. The same is true with you.

5. Most people think success comes without paying the price. Everything that has value has a cost that must be paid. If you want gold, oil or diamonds, you must pay for them. Even obeying the laws of God is a price you pay to become successful. There is a price for discipline and a price for regrets. The price for indiscipline is misery, pain, confusion and lost opportunities.

6. Most people want rewards only. You cannot get a reward and an award when you have not done something. The problem with people is they want to be successful, but never want to do something about it; success then eludes them. Mr. Seth Godin, the author of *Permission Marketing*, says, "You don't win an Olympic gold medal with few weeks of intensive training." Furthermore, Godin adds:

There is no such a thing as an overnight opera sensation. Great law firms or design companies don't spring up overnight... Every great company, every great brand, every great career has been built in the same way: bit by bit, step by step, little by little.

Therefore, success is a process, journey and not an event. It takes time and effort with consistency, persistence and discipline among others.

7. Most people think the successful people are lucky ones. I was born in a poor neighborhood. I became an orphan at age 14; I experienced war and all the setbacks that you can imagine. I decided to make changes in my life and you see me here now I am sharing these ideas. Everyone has ideas. In fact, ideas are the source of wealth, success and prosperity. Some people think others are lucky and it is not true. An Olympic gold medalist never wins out of luck; it comes from hard work, intensive training, and so many factors. Think about it.

8. Most people just hope to succeed. Every day, they have the hope of success. They never plan for it. They never set goals. They keep company with the wrong people. They waste time. They never read any book. They keep complaining. They keep blaming others – parents, friends, spouses and teachers. The worst of all they blame their leaders, government, politicians and the bad weather, climate, etc. Stop all these blame games and renew your mind.

9. Most people success comes because others get opportunities. This might be true, but how do you see opportunities? Some people wait to get opportunities and they never arrive. Opportunities are for those who are ready and prepared. Opportunities come to those who have developed themselves; they have made improvements, acquired knowledge, skills, character, discipline, and attitudes. Some of them say, "If …" The truth is opportunities come to those who do something. If you are a farmer, you will harvest if you work on planting your seeds and do everything that is expected. When the time for harvest comes, you will have the opportunity to reap big time. John Wooden said, "When an opportunity comes, it is too late to prepare." In other words, opportunities come to those who are prepared. Also, opportunities never guarantee that you succeed. They merely give you a starting point or advantage. If you never follow the principles, you still fail.

10. Most people think of right connections to succeed. Social networking is a new concept that has been introduced in recent years. In Uganda, it has even led to social media tax by the government. People are socially networked. Most people go places to network, to meet new people. They exchange contacts, business cards, addresses, phone numbers, e-mails, etc. This is all good. They say you must know someone to get what you want. What you know does not matter, but whom you know does. This is interesting. However, I found these ideas having effects on many people. Whom do you know? What do you know? If you are always looking for people (or the "who"), then you think success comes from connections. However, if you think of what you know, then you are most likely to succeed in your area. I believe the key to success comes from knowing, with knowledge being what you know. Do you know how play football? Do you know accounting, marketing, teaching, selling, baking, writing, planning, organizing or leading? What do you know?

If you are the best at something, you will be successful. The people who believe in connections think if they were coming from the "right" families then they would be successful too. There are those who think their fortune comes from meeting someone who comes from the right family. This is not true. There is nothing wrong with right families, but connections alone cannot bring success. Think of this. If connections were key, then all the kids of rich people would never end up being alcoholics, drug addicts, etc. All the children of pastors, bishops, etc. would be successful. These leaders meet many people and have connections. If you have something unique to give, then you have chances to succeed. The Bible says, "A man's gift makes room for him in the world and will bring him before great people."[9]

11. Most people believe that success is an event. Many people are standing and waiting for the day to come when they will succeed. Let me say this: You will be disappointed. You are going to wait forever. Success is a process, and it is a long journey. Success does not mean the absence of problems, challenges, setbacks and obstacles. Success involves all those things. If you want to experience real change that is sustainable, it will not happen in a moment or instant. It takes time. It is a process. Anything of value is a process. Big companies such as Apple, Samsung, Toyota, Sony, Philips, Coca-Cola, etc. never started yesterday. They started a long time ago before some of the people were born. However, you will find people thinking, "Success will happen. Forget it." You need plans to succeed. You need strategies to succeed. You need ideas and knowledge. You need actions, etc.

12. Most people think of success and failure as things that just happen. I believe success is a result of decisions. Failure is also a result of decisions. By the way, indecision is also a decision. Everybody makes decisions. Those decisions have benefits and costs. They have pros and cons. You cannot blame anyone for something you decided.

---

9   Proverbs 18:16.

If you decide not to work, you know poverty will come to your doorsteps. If you decide to cheat, you know the outcomes. If you dodge classes, lessons, or lectures in high school or college, you know the results. You can predict the outcomes of your life. If you decide to go to the office every day late and possibly anger your boss, you know your future. That is why I say, "Success or failure is a product of decisions." Every decision carries with it outcomes, results that could be positive or negative. Good decisions lead to a good life, but bad ones produce a bad life, too.

Secrets to Success

Many times, people compete and compare themselves with others when it comes to measuring success. My personal views about that include:

- Success must personally be defined by everyone. Decide on what you want to succeed on by performing what you were created to do.

- Success is determined on how you use your time and work on your plans each day.

- Success is a result of decisions. Failure is also a result of decisions. Therefore, successful people make the right decisions and act according to those decisions, but most importantly, they standby and manage their decisions.

- Success is not about the accumulation of property, wealth or things. Instead, it's about pursuing your vision and finishing it.

- Success is a result of preparation. Those who prepare thoroughly win and succeed. Success does not occur to the unprepared.

- Success is a result of becoming valuable. If you become a person of value, then you can attract success.

- The greatest enemy of your success are your past achievements, accomplishments and awards. Your last success and progress can hold you back.

- Success in life doesn't mean absence of problems but bouncing up when you are down.

Chapter 2

ATTITUDE

Your attitude, not your aptitude,
will determine your altitude.
— Zig Ziglar.

The Winner's Attitudes

In my book, *10 Principal Questions of Life: That Successful People Ask and Answer but People Who Fail Ignore and Neglect*, I have extensively written about the importance of attitude in life. As I was reflecting on what I need to write about attitude, I went back to read what I had presented in the book. I did not want to repeat myself. Instead, I wanted to give you new information and insights about the value of positive attitudes.

Let me begin with the quote: "Ideas can change your life. One or more ideas can be a turning point towards your dreams."[10] What is an attitude! Attitude refers to a human predisposition or tendency to respond

---

10   Anonymous.

positively or react negatively towards a certain idea, object, person or situation. Attitude influences an individual's choice of action and responses to challenges, incentives and rewards (collectively called stimuli). The four major components of attitude include:

1. **Affective:** Emotions or feelings.
2. **Cognitive:** Belief or opinions held consciously.
3. **Conative:** Inclination for action.
4. **Evaluative:** Positive or negative response to stimuli.

As we journey together on understanding the power of positive attitude, I have some questions to ask you.

- Is it possible to have a good life without a positive attitude?
- Is it possible to achieve your dreams without a positive attitude?
- Is it possible to succeed in life without a positive attitude?
- Is it possible to have a good relationship without a positive attitude?
- Is it possible to win a competition without a positive attitude?

The answer to all those questions is yes. However, your attitude will have a great bearing on the quality of your life, achievement of your dreams, success in your life, nature of good relationships and winning of the completion. If your attitude is positive, then the ultimate results will be great and powerful.

The Impact of a Negative Attitude

If a person has a poor or negative attitude, there are so many things that will happen. What are those things? You will be able to observe a failure mentality. You will see pessimistic responses to life. You will see skepticism or doubt. You also notice worry or depression. Furthermore, you will notice that an individual is always gloomy, moody or unhappy. People with negative attitude also experience emotional pain and psychological anxiety. They are often overwhelmed by external conditions, situations or circumstances. Their relationships with people are never long-lasting. You must also remember that people with a negative attitude will steal your joy or peace. They criticize others most of the time. They complain almost about everything. They are negative, cynical and judgmental all the time. Do you a close family member, friend or colleague who has a negative attitude? Please, advise them to change their attitude. It is dangerous for both for the relationships.

The writer of *The Strangest Secret*, Earl Nightingale, said, "Our attitude towards others determines their attitude towards us."[11] How we behave towards others will influence their response or reaction to us. Oprah Winfrey was interviewed once and said, "The greatest discovery of all time is that a person can change his future by merely changing his attitude."[12] What does she mean? There are many ways to change the future, but one of them is changing one's attitude. You can choose to have a positive or negative attitude. It is a choice. Everything is a choice.

Why Does Attitude Matter In Life?

There are millions of people endowed with great talents, knowledge, skills, gifts and opportunities. Most of these people die with all these things because they have a bad or negative attitude. They grow but without the right attitude. One example of a person with great talent is Italian professional footballer, Mario Balotelli. This guy has great potential, but his attitude seems wrong. As a result, he has not been able to achieve much more than he is capable. My conclusion is that most of the people who have a bad attitude

11   https://www.brainyquote.com/quotes/earl_nightingale_134690.

12   https://www.brainyquote.com/quotes/oprah_winfrey_387162.

never get very far in life. These people can attain some level of success, but their attitude will bring them down and keep them from maximizing their potential.

However, a person who has a positive attitude even with limited talent, knowledge, skills or gifts can be able to achieve incredible things if they keep and protect their attitude. Thomas Jefferson said, "Nothing can stop the man with the right mental attitude from achieving his goal; nothing on earth can help the man with the wrong mental attitude." I wish I could get that point into your head! Any goal can be achieved if only the attitude is right.

Meanwhile, Viktor E. Frankl said, "Everything can be taken from a man but one thing: the last of human freedoms – to choose one's attitude in any given set of circumstances, to choose one's way."[13] Do you know the story of Victor E. Frankl? This man endured the horrible form of adversity during the Holocaust in Poland when the Nazis executed the evil plan to destroy all Jews. He survived the Holocaust and wrote a book. His advice is simple: You can lose everything, but you must choose the attitude to carry you through life.

As you live your life on Earth, I want you to remember the following facts about attitude:

1. **Attitude determines how tasks and results are completed or achieved.** For any goal to be achieved, there must be a positive attitude. If a football team must win, there must be a right mindset and attitude. The chances of winning or succeeding in any venture increase if the attitude is positive. If the attitude is negative, however, then losing is possible.

---

13   https://www.brainyquote.com/lists/authors/top_10_viktor_e_frankl_quotes.

2. **Attitude is affected by past experiences.** Every person has a share of experiences in life. Some people have past mistakes, past failures and past errors affecting them. Those past events cause them to feel negative or emotional. As a result, they control the people and influence their progress. If you have adverse events that hold you back, then you need to check your attitudes and deal with those events.

3. **Attitude determines how people will treat you in life.** How do people treat you? If you are unhappy always, people will never want to be near you. If you are full of energy, passion, and confidence, you will receive a different kind of treatment. Recently, I met a man in his late 50s in a gym. The guy was full of energy. He was happy. I asked him what was his secret to happiness. He said it was having a positive attitude. What is your attitude towards life? If you put on a tough or combative face or mood, you will receive the same kinds of experiences. But if you put on a happy and smiling face, you will also receive it back. The best way to obtain a proper treatment or response from people is by having a positive attitude.

4. **Attitude can determine your success or failure.** When you compete, what is your overall goal? What do you want to achieve out of it? When you have an exam, what is your motive? I believe the motivation is to succeed or win. A positive attitude not only helps you succeed and win, but also a winner's attitude comes from a positive attitude. Great leaders, business people, athletes, musicians, pastors, doctors, engineers and others all have a positive attitude and winner's mentality. A person or an individual with a positive attitude has something like a secret weapon, useful for fighting a war or battle.

5. **Attitude is a key to happiness, not achievements or accomplishments.** As a young man, I used to think the more I acquire assets, money I make or different places I travel and see, then I would be happy. I did not know I was wrong. Every person is struggling to achieve or accomplish something. All those successes, achievements or accomplishments, however, never make a person happy. Happiness comes from attitude. Attitudes come from your thoughts, not what happens around you or the things around you. Your thoughts are therefore more important than the stuff around you or what happens to you.

6. **Attitude affects those around you.** If a person has negative emotions all the time, then you can tell how those around them feel. To have a positive attitude, you must control what thoughts you are generating or producing from your mind factory. A positive or negative reaction is contagious to the environment where people live: family, office, hospital or community. In every environment or society, there are two categories of people: purifiers and polluters. Purifiers are those who clean up the environment, bring hope, happiness, joy and peace. The polluters, however, are those who destroy the environment and usually the atmosphere changes when they appear. They bring with them "smoke," carbon dioxide and a stuffy environment. The air becomes difficult to breathe. People become suffocated. Polluters have toxic words; where they are, it is difficult to breathe. They make the environment gloomy, dull, negative and contaminated. The purifiers make the situation not only fresh, but also clean. Purifiers are positive people while polluters are negative ones. Always avoid the polluters; otherwise, you will continue to be in a toxic environment, which can suffocate your life.

The Process Of Choosing A Positive Attitude

Everything in life is a matter of choices and decisions. Every person has the willpower to choose. You can select and decide to be positive or negative. Here are some practical actions to take to have a positive attitude:

1. **Take personal responsibility to keep a positive attitude.** There are so many relationships that have failed because one spouse demands the other spouse to make him or her happy. I think this is a tricky thing. Why? Because as we have seen, attitudes come from thoughts. Nobody can control the thoughts of another person. It is not a job or task of a spouse to make the other one happy. It is a personal responsibility. I think one lesson here is that everyone is responsible for his or her attitude. If you want your day, week, month or year to be a happy one, control what you think.

2. **Change your attitude from negative to positive.** Happiness comes from positive thoughts while unhappiness comes from the negative thoughts. The negative thoughts could be from past errors, mistakes, setbacks, failures and regrets.

3. **Know that some things in life cannot be changed.** For instance, the past cannot be changed, but you can create your future. In addition, you cannot choose your parents, where you were born or your race. An attitude is something that you can choose or change through changing or choosing your thoughts.

4. **Decide to change your bad attitude.** If you constantly have negative thoughts, you are going to have a bad life. You should learn this simple message. King Solomon wrote, "As a man thinks

in his heart, so is he."[14] The way you think translates into what you will become. Your thoughts are responsible for producing. Your thoughts shape your actions and that is what you become. If you have been having bad thoughts for the past 10 or 20 years, can you imagine the damage you have caused yourself? Everyone has his or her thoughts. If you want to change your life, then start from the ideas or thoughts created in your mind.

5. **To have a right attitude, life must be appreciated always.** There are many problems that people face daily. These difficulties, hardships or problems cause many thoughts. They cause people to worry, complain and become demotivated. However, the question to the reader is this: Isn't life more important? I believe being alive is a good thing. Many people are healthy but never appreciate the beauty of life. Wait until you are critically ill or hospitalized. Wait until you have a terminal illness. If you never understand life, then you will always have a bad attitude. If you want things to turn around, decide to turn around. John Wooden wrote, "Things turn out best for people who make the best of the way to turn out." That also means if you can change your attitude, then the best will be waiting for you.

How To Manage And Discipline Your Attitude

There many things you can do:

- Every day you must learn to recognize if you have a good or bad attitude.
- Look for positive things in everything or situation.
- Associate with people who have a positive attitude and avoid those

---

with negative reactions. You have heard the saying, "Birds of the same feathers flock together."

- Avoid negative conversations or speaking negatively about situations or issues or complaining.
- Remove completely all negative words that you use daily.
- Be thankful for what you have and appreciate people around you. Say thank you each time and practice the spirit of gratitude.

What My Attitude Has Done in My Life

- My attitude keeps me focused and disciplined.
- My attitude helps me build relationships.
- My attitude always helps me to move out of comfort zones.
- My attitude keeps me struggling and going towards my vision.
- My attitude helps me recover from a crisis of failure.

The Gift of Second Chance

God always gives everyone a chance in life. A second chance means you squandered the first opportunity. Suppose you have been living a miserable life because of bad attitude. Now you have seen why positivity matters. You must take this information as a second chance. If your attitude in the past has not been good, then you have been given a second chance. You can choose to have a right attitude. You can decide to manage your attitude every day. If you manage and choose your attitude, then you will be open to new opportunities and possibilities.

*Your attitude is a key
to new opportunities
and possibilities.*

Chapter 3

BIG-HEARTEDNESS

In a time of domestic crisis, men of goodwill and generosity
should be able to unite regardless of party or politics.
— John F. Kennedy

What Is Big-Heartedness?

Have you heard someone say, "That person has a big heart"? A big-hearted person is kind or generous. They demonstrate a life of kindness or generosity. The words below make sense to me. I do not know about you, but I think they truly reflect the nature of mankind.

The Paradoxical Commandments

"People are illogical, unreasonable, and self-centered.
Love them anyway.

If you do good, people will accuse you of selfish ulterior motives.
Do good anyway.

If you are successful, you will win false friends and true enemies.
Succeed anyway.

The good you do today will be forgotten tomorrow.
Do good anyway.

Honesty and frankness make you vulnerable.
Be honest and frank anyway.

The biggest men and women with the biggest ideas can be shot down by the
smallest men and women with the smallest minds.
Think big anyway.

People favor underdogs but follow only top dogs.
Fight for a few underdogs anyway.

What you spend years building may be destroyed overnight.
Build anyway.

People really need help but may attack you if you do help them.
Help people anyway.

Give the world the best you have and you'll get kicked in the teeth.
Give the world the best you have anyway."[15]

---

15   Kent M. Keith, *The Silent Revolution: Dynamic Leadership in the Student Council*

How Kindness Costed Me $ 5,000?

When I think about those words in the last section, it reminds me that it is simply not easy to please people. It is not easy to be kind or generous, but as humans, we must continue to stay on course with the motive to assist those less fortunate in our society. There is saying, "Charity begins at home." There is no way you can help or be kind to others when it does not start from home. However, you must remember that your kindness can be a blessing or a curse. To me kindness or generosity brings you significance. It brings hope to the hopeless and sometimes changes the lives of those who are unfortunate. Kindness can also cause pain. It can cost the kind person so much in terms of relationship mishaps, losses and other problems.

I vividly recall a time when I received an international phone call about a pending arrest to me for a case that I never created. The magistrate had ruled a case against me and I was required to pay $5,000. In Africa, that is a lot of money and it takes me over two months to raise that money. What was the matter? What caused that problem? It was my kindness. Let me tell you the story. I had employed one of my relatives in my project. He was the overall supervisor. I was out of the country when my cousin was running the show or the project. When I returned after a long absence, I received very disturbing information about my manager – my cousin – and there was evidence of misconduct, harassment and bad behavior that warranted me to take an action to terminate him. I received several insights about the unbecoming or bad conduct, methods of work and general attitude of my cousin. As some of you might have predicted, I simply ignored the information. I spoke to my cousin with humility and requested him to stop all bad behavior and harassment of workers.

When I left the project, my cousin never followed my advice; instead, he terminated the workers. The workers were dissatisfied and decided to go to court. They opened a case and we tried to negotiate a settlement out of court and failed. They pursued the case and we lost it. When I was informed about the court judgment, I concluded that my kindness was the cause of that problem. I think I should have terminated my cousin and save my name. Kindness is good but can be costly. Just learn the lessons of life when you meet such experiences.

A Gift of $25

Some years back I was working in Adamawa State in Nigeria. I lived in one of the hotels for over four months. It was difficult to get accommodation. The longer I stayed in that hotel, the more I got used to the hotel workers. There was a young lady whom I shall call "Flora" (which is not her real name). She worked as one of the managers in the hotel. I got to know her as a humble and disciplined person. She was quiet, honest and hardworking. She was also time-conscious. I learned that she had a similar background like mine with a humble beginning. She planned of continuing her university education, but she had no way out as the parents were unable to help. Still, I spoke to her about the benefit of going to college and I inspired her. She finally worked hard to be admitted to one of the state universities.

After about a year, she started a course at the university. She informed me that she had commenced her studies and was happy with it. She said that I inspired her to go back to college after I left Nigeria. She also said that I left an impact on her and she keeps on remembering everything I told her, and her resolution was that she was not going to surrender or give up. One evening, she sent a WhatsApp message saying that she was facing a financial difficulty. She said she was going back to join her family to get financial support. So, I asked her how much money did she want? She said, 8,000 Naira, which is the equivalent of $25. I replied a message to her to wait as I speak to my Nigerian friend, Mr. Samuel. O. Adeyemi of Media DNA, Lagos Nigeria. My good friend was able to assist Flora with 8,000 Naira. She received the money, sent an appreciation and continued with her studies. What lessons can you learn from that story? You do not have to be rich to be kind or generous. What is needed is a heart that is willing to assist. The principle is give what you can afford cheerfully.

The Benefits Of Big-Heartedness

Everything in life has benefits and costs, advantages and disadvantages. Everything has pros and cons. And so it is with big-heartedness. If you are kind or generous, you will enjoy some of the privileges in which I will discuss. But first, let start with some questions. How much are you willing to give out to others from your income? Whom should you help? Do you know of people who are generous in your family or community? If you are not willing to give, then the Bible says you are a greedy. Greed is a sin and God hates it and all sins.

As you think about being big-hearted, here are four main benefits of giving, generosity or kindness, including the following:

- **Giving allows you the opportunity to influence people:** A person who influences others is always the leader. Leadership is the capacity of influencing others to achieve common goals. If a person has a big heart, that person is likely to influence the destiny of the people receiving assistance. I have experienced this and seen that the people who give away always continue to lead others. For instance, Bill Gates started a charity foundation that has been able to assist millions of people around the world. Because of Bill Gates' desire to assist needy people suffering from HIV/ AIDS, Malaria and poverty in various parts of the world, he has received another opportunity to influence people through his wife and his organization. You might think that I have used an example of one of the richest people on planet. If you look around your community, you will realize that a person who gives or assists people during times of crises or problems is respected and honoured.

However, a greedy person does not always have a slight chance to influence others. People are attracted to a person who is a giver. I could list generous and greedy people that I know, but I will respect them. Your main task is to know that giving will give you an opportunity to lead and serve others.

- **Giving enable you to focus on what's on the outside rather than the inside:** A generous person does not always give to himself or herself; instead, they focus on the people outside. For over 15 years, I assisted relatives and orphans. I never focused on myself. The impact of focusing on others helped to appreciate what it means to humankind. I believe one of the greatest responsibilities every human must perform on Earth is giving to others in need. I recall a time again when my maternal aunt was sick from terminal cancer with no way out of it. The family was shattered; all resources had been used to try to save my aunt. I contributed money to assist her and it brought hope to the family. I have learned that people always remember the little acts of kindness that you give. I remember assisting my aunts and how it greatly benefited them.

- **Giving saves and improves people's lives and conditions:** If you look at the lives of the people that receive assistance, you will notice changes. For example, I helped build a simple structure for some people. For people who slept in grass-thatched huts their entire lives, the simple act of building a house for them changed their lives forever. In another example, I spent years educating my own family, siblings and relatives. I had a lot of responsibility and I had to spend a lot of resources educating these people from high school through college and university. As a matter of fact, when they finished their education, their lives were no longer the same. Some of them have been able to have job opportunities that they would not have had if I had not supported them. I am also a product of someone's act of kindness. My education was a result of external help, and without it, I would not be where I am today. Decide to give to others.

- **Giving brings value to the giver and the receiver:** I also believe that kindness benefits those who give and those receive. There is some value that is gained through giving. I noticed that every time a person gives assistance to others, they become happy and joyful. I recall an evening when I visited a mother of one of friends. I had carried a loaf of bread and sugar. This sounds like a small gift, but when I gave the items, I could feel the joy and happiness from the old woman. There was another time when I gave my spouse money to buy gifts to old people at my mother's birthplace. So, my wife went to Owino Market in Kampala and spent about $300 for the Christmas gifts. When we delivered the items, all the people were very happy. Something interesting happened three months after that incident. There was a Thanksgiving ceremony in our home for accomplishing my doctorate from Regent University in Virginia in the United States of America. I received overwhelming gifts from my uncles, aunts and friends that shocked me. Even the people that I never expected to give gave as little as $1 or $2 among others. I believe that they gave out of their hearts and out of genuine love. The more you give, the more you will experience an increase or abundance. The less you give, the less your value.

- **Giving brings glory to God:** If you are a believer in God, then you might have heard, "God loves a cheerful giver."[16] Further, it says, "Each of you should give what you have decided in your heart to give, not reluctantly or under compulsion, for God loves a cheerful giver."[17] Giving attracts God's love to the giver. The reverse is true. If you are not a giver, you cannot attract God's love. The point is that you must learn to give, and you will be blessed throughout your life.

- **Giving inspires the giver:** I would like you to imagine the joy that you see on the faces of people whose lives were transformed because of your generosity. Can you picture the happiness? When you give assistance to people, you will be inspired. The inspiration comes from the fact you have changed the lives of others. You cannot put a dollar on that act. It brings fulfillment and satisfaction. I can imagine, Jesus Christ after feeding 5,000 families on the shores of Galilee. He must have been a happy person.

---

16   2 Corinthians 9:7.
17   Ibid.

What Should You Give To Others?

If you have agreed with my concepts about giving, then I want us to take the conversation to the next level. Some people think that you can only give money, which is what most people want. This is not true. There are many things that you can give and let the people take it or reject it. When I made a commitment and decision to become kind and generous, I decided that I was going to give to those who want my help in any of the following situations:

1. **Give advice to people:** Sometimes, people don't want money from you; all they want is advice. As you live in today's world, you are going to experience pain, disappointments, setbacks, challenges, problems and many things that hurt you. In those moments, your problem might not be food, money or cars, but it might turn out that you need advice. Giving a person advice can save you. I remember sitting with a friend named Patricia. I was going through difficult times and she gave a simple advice. It worked miracles and changed my life. So, do not refuse to give advice to those who need or ask for it.

2. **Give information and knowledge:** You might know the adage, "Information is power." Is this statement true? To some extent, it is true. In today's world, information has become more critical than anything. It is more powerful. Its power has given people opportunities. I remember one of my friends gave me information about a job opportunity when I had just completed university. I was looking for a job and that information helped me get a job afterwards. Because of that job, my siblings and relatives were able to get an education. I was able to earn income that I used to pay fees or tuition.

3. **Give money if you have it:** I have known people who think their money is everything. They are never willing to give it out to others. I believe they are totally wrong. I know of a family where money is everything. There was a time when the man of the house lost a job and the family was struggling financially. I got the information I decided to send them assistance and it saved them from being evicted by the landlord, but the irony is that later, this man managed to secure a stable job. Even though the family now has stable sources of incomes, they fear losing jobs or giving money to others because money is everything. I learned as a Christian that nothing is permanent or lasts forever. My principle has always been to give to those who need help. Andrew Carnegie said, "No man can enrich himself, unless he enriches others." To me, this statement carries heavy responsibilities and is true. If you enrich others, you will influence them; they will trust you to lead them. You will become a leader.

4. **Give your time:** Time is a precious commodity. Everyone has 24 hours in a day. You need to give people part of your time. Be there for them. Be available. Sometimes people just want your presence. Your presence can cause change in the destiny of others. Suppose you a leader and you need to give your followers time to tell you the problems or issues they are facing. When you listen to them, you might find solutions that help set people free.

5. **Give your experiences:** Every person has a story. It can be a good or bad one. It does not matter. People often learn through the stories of others. Your story could become an inspiration to another person. If you met me physically or through this book, you will know my life's story. I believe what I have done on Earth is because of my own experiences.

6. **Give yourself:** The last thing to give is yourself. You need to be willing to pay the price to help others. I believe that Jesus Christ gave Himself for His friends. In addition, the Bible says, "For even the Son of Man did not come to be served, but to serve, and to give his life as a ransom for many."[18] Are you willing to give up yourself? What have you done for your friends?

How Do You Develop the Culture of Giving?

The value of giving others grows from childhood. It is manifested when a person becomes an adult. I grew up in two places: my father's and mother's birthplaces in Bukedea (formerly Kumi). I observed what my parents and grandparents did. I will share some of those ideas:

1. **Love and value people as yourself:** To be a giver, you must value and love people.

2. **Make people more important than what you give:** Everyone needs dignity, respect and love. If you want to give, then let the people become more important than the things of the world. People are more important than earthly things and that is the reason why God gave man to take charge of the Garden of Eden.

3. **Become more valuable:** You cannot give without having value. You need to give. Giving comes from having something. The more you become valuable, the more your capacity increases to give.

4. **Learn to accept people as they are:** The poor and rich have one thing in common: The grave is our destiny. Know that you cannot take away the accumulated wealth, riches or things with you.

---

18   Mark 10: 45.

5. **Stop waiting to give; start now:** You do not need to have much to give, but give whatever you can or have. Every day you have the gift of life. You can give any of the gifts I listed above.

6. **Think of the reasons why must give:** We all have motives each day. Our motives must serve to the interest of humanity.

7. **People remember your giving:** Giving is a simple act, but it never is forgotten. My Aunt Elizabeth's late husband, Mr. Benjamin Okia, was a humble man and a giver. I cannot forget his humble nature. Whenever I visit my aunt, I recall Uncle Benjamin. He is gone but never forgotten. His works and deeds are still living on Earth. His testimony is still fresh.

8. **Teach others the value of giving:** The duty of parents and teachers is guide, mentor and train children. A person's goal must be to teach children to give. Can you imagine the benefits of kindness? They far outweigh the benefits of selfishness or greed.

Chapter 4

COMMITMENT

The only limit to your impact
is your imagination and commitment.
— Tony Robbins

Does Commitment Matter Really?

That question was asked to me one evening when some friends and I were getting out of the United Nations compound for physical exercise. I thought about that question and realized there are so many things in which we humans always find ourselves getting involved (for instance, starting relationships, family, good health, going back to college, building a home, starting a company, starting a school or health center, raising children, supporting a cause or a movement, participating in development projects and many others). I have learned that unless you are committed fully to accomplish something, it is not possible to finish what you start doing.

One of the things that my mentor told us was this: "It is more beneficial and important to be faithful than being famous." That is something that also caught me off guard. I wrote that statement in my journal so that it would remind me about it each time I opened my journal. I knew there are so many distractions that cause vital information or ideas to get lost in the middle the daily things that happen in life. Bad news always dominates; good news still rarely makes it into the public from the media.

*It is more beneficial and important
to be faithful than being famous.*

Let me give an example. If I got 20,000 dollars and went to the bank to deposit it to my account in my country, the act of banking that sum of money would never become news at all on the front page of the newspaper. Suppose, however, a robber uses a rifle or a gun to rob that amount from a commercial bank. Then, all the headlines of papers would be reporting about the robbery incident. Now, the habit of writing any concept that appears useful to me was introduced to me by one of my professors, Dr. David Fraser, who also mentored me at the master's degree level at Uganda Christian University. I have come to appreciate it over the years. Can you imagine opening an old diary or journal only to see the information or idea that you wrote in it? It is a good thing. It is easy to forget what is important and focus on what is less important.

What Is Commitment?

The concept of commitment is about having an agreement to do something. It is a pledge of undertaking to do something regardless of the cost or how much it will demand. For instance, if you commit to improve education, then you do not stop until education standards are developed. If you wish to engage in good leadership, then you never settle for bad leadership.

Some words are related or "cousins" to commitment. To me, I think of faithful, devotion or loyal. I believe you use any of those words to describe some of your friends. I have a list friends (Moses Ojota, Simon Anguria, Moses Bwire and others) with whom I can associate those words. When I try to predict the lifestyle of those guys, I can tell what they are doing even when they are not with me or when I am thousands of miles or kilometers away. I think the degree of my trust for them is 99.99% or even 100%. Sometimes, I think that commitment has its roots in self-discipline, character and vision. A person who has self-discipline, integrity and ideas has the potential for commitment. Regardless of the conditions or circumstances, they become faithful, loyal or devoted to a cause and never think of quitting.

A person who has self-discipline, character and vision has the potential for commitment.

Some Of The Causes Of Problems

As human beings living on Earth, we encounter challenges, problems and setbacks. When you assess the roots of some of our hardships, you will realize that they are internally or externally generated. For instance, someone commits to smoking, drinking or other dangerous behaviors. I think those who smoke or drink heavily become committed to that. I recall a couple of classmates from to school years ago. They used to go to drink in a bar behind Wandegeya Post Office in Kampala. Other friends used to go to drink at a place that was in Bugolobi called Windows. These guys were very faithful and committed to the point that every Friday through Sunday, they *had* to go to those places. I believe they were determined and the outcomes were not all good for some. I recall some got involved in some relationships that eventually cost them their lives.

What makes me sad, however, is that those friends died with all their potential. What is potential? Potential is a hidden gift, talent, or ideas and dreams that await to be manifested. In my book, *Success Principles: Proven Secrets for Achieving Your Dreams and Vision,* there is a complete chapter of the concept of potential. It is an excellent piece to read. However, some of us who were committed to other social and spiritual activities such as fellowship, prayer meetings and church missions also took us to different directions. I believe with all my heart that everybody was born for a reason. God created us to be fruitful, multiply and dominate the earth. Accomplishing that assignment requires commitment. There is no way any person can achieve much in life without commitment.

Why People Never Keep Their Commitments

One of the things to know is that your commitment level will be tested or attacked daily (for instance, a commitment to work, lead or help those that need assistance). Your commitment to happiness, peace, and relationships among others will be tested or attacked. Your commitment to integrity, self-discipline, honesty, faith, values and principles will also be tested or attacked. Commitment is not an event, but rather a process. It's something that must become a part of your life.

*Commitment level will be tested
or attacked daily.*

How do you become excellent in keeping commitments? To keep your commitments, you must be a person who upholds values and principles. Let us be honest; commitment demands the following:

- Be prepared to stand alone.
- Be ready for failure.
- Be willing to learn.
- Be prepared for attacks.
- Be prepared for distractions.
- Be prepared for challenges.

Why Must Commitment Be Kept?

Before I dive into the reasons for keeping commitments, I would like to ask you some questions. Do you know your purpose in life? Do you think you can achieve your life's goals? Do you know where you are heading to in life? What kind of legacy do you want to leave behind? Do you want to lead and influence others? Do you want better relationships? If your answer to those questions is yes, then you need more dosage of a commitment than another person who answered no. Every person has the potential to make a lasting impact and contribution, but they often misuse their potential. Achieving a personal purpose always requires total commitment. Your quality of commitment has a direct relationship with the quality of your life. Now, commitment matters because of the following:

1. **Commitment can improve and change your life.** Suppose you have set goals to keep good health after the doctors said your smoking or drinking habits are unhealthy and are likely to destroy your life. Then out of that message, you decide to abandon all those vices that can cause you bad health. What do you think would happen? You have high chances of improving and even changing your life. I know some friends who used to be alcoholics, but during my interaction with them, they started drinking tea like me, and today, they have completely enjoyed an improvement in their lives. Some people have regrets in life at some point in life. It is a fact that something you cannot change, but there are those things that you can change. Change those things you can and leave those for which you are unable to change to God.

2. **Commitment enables you to avoid some challenges or obstacles in life.** Every person living on Earth has problems whether it is the President of the United States, China, Russia or beggars in the streets of any African city. The day you die is when you cease to have problems. Problems are part of the game called life. If problems are part of life, then how are you going to overcome problems? Some people have formulas such as avoiding, transferring, studying, assessing, examining, imagining or solving the problems. All these are ways in which people deal with or overcome obstacles. Some people confront issues. Some people run away. Some people hide. Some people ignore or neglect. One approach to avoiding the potential impact of the issues or obstacles is by being committed. Commitment can save a person from some issues.

3. **Commitment helps in attainment of higher-level goals or purpose in life.** At the beginning of this chapter, I made a statement that commitment has "cousin" words such as devotion or faithful. Many people often start things, relationships and projects. Starting them is quite easy; however, staying faithful or committed to the end is a challenge. Most people give up, give in or surrender. The only formula or decision to make before giving up, giving in or surrendering is staying committed. How many people do you know who gave up when they were about to win?

4. **Commitment produces leaders.** If you can keep your commitments, then there are high chances that you will become a power of influence. If you are known for lack of commitment, however, nobody will entrust you for any leadership position. I think people who lack commitment, can also lack self-motivation, self-discipline or lack of self-drive. Once you are committed to

something and set some goals, then you have a great possibility of achieving them. Commitments creates trusts and great relationships.

The Strategies For Keeping Commitments

We have explored the significance of commitments. How does one, on the other hand, ensure commitments are maintained. The following prepositions are offered:

1. **Determine the cost and benefits of commitments.** Everything will cost you. Some things will benefit you.

2. **Decide to pay the price.** If the price is high, then you should keep the commitments. Once you have known and determined the cost, then you must estimate what you want to lose or gain.

3. **Do your best to pursue excellence.** When I was in Mbale High School, our motto was: "Whatever you do, do it well." This statement is a principle of life. It is talking about excellence. If anyone desires to be successful and effective, then they must ensure they are committed all the time. The best Japanese companies have workers who are committed to excellence. They have no provision for mediocre performance.

4. **Remember that keeping commitments is never easy.** It is a daily struggle. Everything that I have achieved or done in life, I managed it because of God's grace and my commitment. There were times I felt like giving up, but when I remember the cost, then I get inspired, motivated and encouraged to keep on keeping on. There are, however, some friends whom I know lost commitment when setbacks confronted them.

5. **Never rely on your natural gifts alone.** You must rely on your values, principles and standards. Some people use talents to achieve what they want, but talent alone is not sufficient in keeping commitments. If you want to win a gold medal at the Olympics, you require both commitment and talent among others.

> ***Winning = Commitment + Talent***
> ***+ Other variables.***

6. **Commitment requires being single-minded.** Double-minded people never keep commitments.

7. **Commitment requires that you strive to do what is right always with self-discipline.** One of the greatest battles in life is keeping self-discipline and summoning the energy for hard work to create desired results. Working hard pays, but working smartly brings results and paycheck.

Integrity and Commitment

It has been said that integrity is being true to your words and actions. It is never easy to keep your words. Making promises is easy, but keeping promises is hard. How many people make promises but never keep them? If you have integrity, you will keep your promises and your commitments. If you do not have integrity, you only keep commitments when it is convenient for you. If you are committed to something, however, then you will have no reasons to give and only deliver results.

Benefits That I Got From My Commitment

Whenever I think of my commitments, I realized what I got out of it. Some of the benefits from my commitment include the following:

- My commitment helped me gain knowledge, skills and competencies.
- My commitment helped me learn and get experience.
- My commitment motivated me to finish what I started and never to give up.
- My commitments kept me going, never giving up or quitting even when things got difficult or hardships came my way.
- My commitments have pushed me from my comfort zone to pursue my purpose.
- My commitment has inspired many people.

If there is a takeaway lesson for the person reading, your commitments combined with determination will be critical in life. If you work hard enough, you will find a way. If you are committed and determined, you will have results without reasons.

*If you are committed and determined,
you will have results without reasons.
Your commitment will give you tenacity
or persistence.*

Chapter 5

COMMUNICATION

Wise men speak because they have something to say;
fools because they have to say something.
– Plato

How Relationships Are Established

How do people on Earth relate or interact with each other? I believe one-way in which people live harmoniously together is through communication based on understanding. Understanding allows people to create relationships and the lack of it creates conflicts or tension. When there is misunderstanding, then communication has not been effective. All communication brings people to a commonplace where they can understand each other. Communication occurs when two or more people understand each other, agree to work together or agree on common issues. When people are on the common ground of understanding each other, then there is tremendous power that is built and generated.

At the turn of the new century, the inventors and innovators created different modes of communication that have revolutionized the way information is transmitted. Communication can be one-way or two-way. Social media platforms such as Facebook, Twitter, LinkedIn and others have also been useful in sharing information. The benefits and costs of using the social media will be experienced with time. Researchers have estimated that an average American spends about 9 hours a day on social media.

If success, prosperity and advancement are to be attained, then there must be loving human relationships glued together by communication. It is impossible to have excellent human relations without communicating. Relationships blossom when there is communication; they dry when there is no communication. Therefore, communication is a vital aspect of human life. It is a foundation for human relations and brings people closer together to pursue common interests and goals. People work together if there is communication but fail to progress when there is a communication breakdown or gap. The advancement in human relations only happens when people have reached common ground and can understand all aspects of information conveyed or transmitted.

As you will see, I will present various types of relationships in Chapter 11 (such as the associations existing among household members, business partners and corporate members). Understand this for now: The only way those relations are sustained is through communication. It is not easy to communicate or transmit information. Some people have difficulties communicating with each other. It practically means they fail to build relationships. Some people are either good or bad at communication. An excellent communicator quickly makes relationships. A lousy communicator, on the other hand, often finds it difficult to influence or convince people.

Some people are good at presenting their ideas, views and opinions while others are terrible, not good at all.

When people fail to reach a common ground, they start to pull each other. It is like a contest, a fight or a battle. The winner of the battle carries the day. The best ways to communicate effectively are finding common ground and practicing communicating. Jim Rohn said, "Take advantage of every opportunity to practice your communication skills so that when important occasions arise, you will have the gift, the style, the sharpness, the clarity, and the emotions to affect other people."[19] There are many things that every person can learn because each person has billions of brain cells. Each brain can absorb a massive volume of information.

If there is one thing that is key to success, then it is communication. One of the keys to success in life on Earth is communication. Without better expertise in communication, it is impossible to influence others. Those who communicate well always influence others. They are capable of emerging as leaders. Now, leadership has been said to be the capacity to influence others to achieve common goals. Influence only occurs when there is effective communication. Effective communication facilitates the building of relationships and hence affecting others.

What Makes Communication Difficult?

Many things affect or make communication difficult. Some of these things include:
- Attitude towards others.
- Perception.
- Ego.
- Words used.
- Tone.

19   https://www.success.com/rohn-the-4-building-blocks-of-good-communication/

- What is said and when it is said.
- Body language.
- Timing.
- Acceptance of the message.
- Interpretation.

Strategies for Becoming an Excellent Communicator

The following can be useful for anyone with an aspiration to become an excellent communicator:

- Become a good listener.
- Make people feel comfortable with you.
- Respond only when deemed necessary.
- Read extensively and keep learning to widen your knowledge base.
- Do not imitate others but be yourself.
- Practice, practice, practice.

Skills Needed for Effective Communication

- Reading.
- Writing.
- Speaking.
- Listening.

The final point I want to make here is that all the skills of communication can be learned. The choice is always yours. Also, remember that without good communication, you cannot adequately establish good relations or lead others as a leader. Leaders are readers; that is why they must master of the art or science of communication.

Chapter 6

FAITH

Believe in yourself! Have faith in your abilities!
Without a humble but reasonable confidence in your own
powers you cannot be successful or happy.
*— **Norman Vincent Peale***

Faith Is Key During Changing Times And Seasons Of Life

I believe that faith holds the key to life's meaning, and without it, we surrender, and the devil comes to destroy and kill and steal our plans, ideas and dreams. We lose direction when faith is lost or misplaced. We lose hope when faith is lost. We lose the future when faith is lost. Due to the temporary challenges of today, we lose the opportunities that are ahead when faith is lost. So, faith is a master key.

Life is a journey of ups and downs as well as good and bad moments. The success of that journey depends on your faith, character, persistence, discipline, values and resilience. We have God on our side. Everything that happens God sees the heart. God has not left us. God is still. God promises us both seasons. God promises us that He will be with us to the end. The difficulties of today will not last. Nothing is permanent except God, His promises, His Word, laws, commandments, principles, change and time. I pray that no decision is taken because of pressure or pain, but we rejoice every day because God has given us just a new day. I thank God every day. I commit each day and future to Him in prayer.

The Value Of Faith In My Life:

This is what I have found to be the benefits of my faith:

- In my teenage years, faith gave me hope for eternal life and enabled me to overcome tragedy.
- In my 20s, faith gave me courage and confidence.
- In my 30s, faith gave me the grace to help others.
- In my 40s, faith is giving me the foundation for leadership and influence. Faith is giving me hope that my vision is possible.
- Moreover, I believe in my 50s, faith will continue to help me with leadership and will give me peace. I believe that no one can give you peace except faith in God. I am going to continue making faith to be at the center of everything I do.

The Power of Faith

If there is one thing that each human needs to develop and acquire on earth, then it should be faith. It should be your spirituality or belief system. Faith is necessary; because of faith, it serves as a measure of how much you can acquire in life. The quantity and quality of your faith determine how much you can achieve in life. If you have weak faith, then there is a likelihood that you might not achieve that much. Whereas if you have strong faith, then you have also an equal chance of attaining more. Your faith is your belief. Where is your faith? Where have you placed your beliefs? Some people have put their faith in people, friends, properties, families, power, wealth, riches and all those things that we consider valuable.

However, one of the lessons that Jesus taught His disciples was that they should put their faith in God.[20] Your faith should not be placed in any of those things that I listed above. The main reason is to protect yourself from pain, disappointment or loss. When you lose any of those, you can lose your own life. However, if your faith is in God, you know that God is omnipotent, the Almighty and strong. There are four types of beliefs that I have come to appreciate and apply in my own life:

- Belief in big dreams, vision, ideas, and plans.
- Belief in me.
- Believe in my mission and purpose.
- Belief in a few trustworthy friends.
- Belief in God's power.

What are your belief systems? In what do you believe? Do you believe in what people have told you? Have you accepted the opinion of others? Let me say the truth: What have you believed for years has either made you either progressive or not. It has either limited you or allowed you to fly higher. I know someone who believed in the lies or opinions of some. They accepted the opinion of those around them. They believed in those lies, and finally, they found themselves heading nowhere. They accepted the lies as "truth," which resulted in their 'imprisonment of the mind." What they accepted as 'truth' was a total lie or wrong views.

Jesus said, "Then you will know the truth, and the truth will set you free."[21] If you get to the point in your life in which you know or discover

---

20   Mark11:22.
21   John 8:32.

the truth, then that truth will give you complete freedom. However, if you are ignorant of the truth, then you are in total darkness or imprisonment. I recall years ago as a young Christian; I never knew much about God until when I got to know the truth. That knowledge of the truth separated me from all the wrong ideas, opinions or information that I had received about me.

Now the problem with humanity is how and where to get the truth. What is your source of truth? Where do you go to get the truth? Your source of truth must come from God, the manufacturer who created you, but not the people who never created you. The only person who knows the truth about a product is the one who made the product. You are like a product, created or manufactured by a company. Samsung only knows the capacity, potency and purpose of the products made by Samsung. The same principle is related to human beings that God created in His image. To know the truth, you must return to God.

Remember in Genesis, the rebellious act or sin by Adam separated humankind from God. To get reconciled requires going to the mediator between man and God, who is Jesus Christ. If two parties have parted ways without any reconciliation, then a mediator must be a third person who can bring the two together. Jesus Christ is the mediator because His sacrificial death on the cross led to washing, cleansing and attornment of human sins. That process enables humankind again to take the nature of God's image—Holy, because the Holy Spirit returns and dwells in the body again, through accepting Jesus as Lord and Savior. Also, Jesus answered, "I am the way and the truth and the life. No one comes to the Father except through me."[22] What does this answer mean? Do you recall the question about the source of truth? If your source of truth is not Jesus, then you need to recheck it.

---

22   John 14: 6.

Faith Defined

Hebrews 11:1 says, "Now faith is confidence in what we hope for and assurance about what we do not see." The writer of Hebrews says that faith is the confidence or assurance that we have or hope of what we do not see. Suppose you have a dream, a vision or a plan, you could see it and have a hope of getting to realize your dream, reach to your vision or attain your plan. The confidence and assurance give you hope or makes you hopeful with certainty is faith. There are different ways in which people respond to things in life as follows:

- Some people wish for things.
- Some people wait for things.
- Some people dream of things.
- Some people hope for things.
- Some people plan for things.
- Some people make things.

So many years ago, I was among the people who wished, waited, dreamed and hoped for things. It was not until I started to plan, however, that I started to see things become a reality. Before I started planning, everything looked impossible. Planning gave me the confidence that I would achieve whatever I wished, waited, wanted, dreamed or hoped. It was at this point that I concluded that planning is the same as faith and faith is the same as planning.

In the Bible says, "For I know the plans I have for you," declares the LORD, "plans to prosper you and not to harm you, plans to give you hope and a future."[23] Who knows the plans? Who has the plans? From the above Scripture, it says that only the Lord knows the plans for everything you

---

23 Jeremiah 29:11

hope and about the future you dream. Now if you have faith in God, then God can show you the content of the plans He has for you. He knows the big picture, but God will not show you everything. He will show you pieces or bits through dreams, desires, ideas, visions or revelations. If God showed you everything required to get to your dreams, you could become terrified, scared or afraid to go forward.

Let me illustrate with two examples. First, with the story of Joseph in Genesis 37, Joseph saw two dreams or visions that were related and connected to him helping and leading his family. However, God never showed him how he was going to fulfill the dream. God never showed him where the dreams or visions would be fulfilled or even when. He never even showed him that his brothers would become angry with him, attempt to kill him, throw him in a pit, sell him to trade merchants and that he would end up in jail because of false accusations by the Pharaoh's wife. Joseph never saw or glanced at all the difficulties, problems, challenges and setbacks that he faced. Joseph never knew that he would be separated or isolated from his parents. He never knew he would be on his own for a long time before the dream became a reality.

The second example is God promised Abraham that he would become a father of many nations. This message was passed to Abraham when he already of advanced age (Genesis 17, 18 &19). However, how long did that vision of being a father of many nations come to pass? God fulfilled the vision by giving Abraham a son named Isaac; then Isaac had two sons, Jacob and Esau; Jacob gave birth to twelve sons that became the twelve sons of Israel. Abraham, Isaac, Jacob, and the sons of Jacob all died before seeing the vision that God gave to Abraham. God works through generations to fulfill His will and purpose. The reason visionaries have confidence is that they know how vision gets fulfilled. A vision can never be achieved without faith. You need faith to pursue the vision. That is why God loves people who have faith because they will be able to see the vision come to pass.

Furthermore, the Bible says, "And without faith, it is impossible to please God because anyone who comes to him must believe that he exists and that he rewards those who earnestly seek him."[24] There are many examples of leaders in the Bible who also received a vision but went through various challenges to reach it. Even in our world, people such as Abraham Lincoln, Nelson Mandela, Mahatma Gandhi, Mother Teresa and others took years to have their visions or dreams fulfilled.

What Do I Learn About Faith?

Faith means waiting for or on God to act. Faith means patience with God. You cannot hurry God to do something. Whenever God gives a vision, a promise, idea or a dream, then the bearer must wait for it through action. Paul said, "Faith without action is dead." You must act to manifest a vision. Look at the examples of Joseph or Abraham; they did something that made them realize their vision. For Joseph, he paid the price of jail, rejection and suffered humiliation. Joseph also interpreted dreams while in prison, which made him get the appointment as a planner or a leader to manage a crisis of famine in Egypt. He also used his knowledge, talents and gifts to achieve his vision. What knowledge, talent or vision are you not using to achieve the dreams you have been holding onto for 20 or 30 years now? Another example is the story of a message about Jesus that was delivered to Mary by Angel Gabriel. It took nine months for the baby to be born.

Faith is nothing but waiting on God to act according to His will and purpose. However, waiting requires something we human beings hate. We hate the word patience. Being patient means you can wait. That also means that faith is patience. When you have faith, you have patience, but when

---

24 Hebrew 11: 6

you lose faith, even the patience disappears. A person who loses faith also loses patience. They fail the waiting test. Faith is thus the patience to wait for God. It can be nine months, 25 years or 4 generations. Can we wait for that long when God gives us a vision? How long can we wait? One thing about people is that generally don't like waiting. People never have the grace to wait. When they have a plan, a dream or vision, they want it to happen fast or now. The primary reason why people never achieve their dreams is that they lack the patience or ability to stay steady during the waiting period.

Why Does Faith Matter In Life?

There are many reasons that I can list as the significance of faith. These reasons are my personal ones and you might have your own reasons.

- Faith gives confidence in life.
- Faith gives hope.
- Faith gives power and victory.
- Faith destroys and neutralizes fear.
- Faith helps to understand the mysteries of life.
- Faith gives the capacity to have a divine perspective.
- Faith gives health.
- Faith gives strengths.
- Faith gives resilience.
- Faith gives courage.
- Faith gives peace.
- Faith indicates man's limited power and knowledge.

Where Is Your Faith?

Jesus asked this question to the disciples each time there was a crisis. I believe everyone has faith in someone or something. The faith comes from information or experiences. Suppose you are having a health problem. You go to see a physician who examines you and gives you a prescription to buy drugs to take for a period. You take the medicine and complete it. What does this mean? It means you have faith in the doctor. What about when you go to your office and you have the office chair that you use during your work. When you sit in it, you have faith in that chair. However, the problem with faith in things and people is that things change just as people change. True faith must not be in things or people but God. Even if we have beliefs, the faith must remain in God.[25]

How To Protect Your Faith

Based on several years of constant work and pursuit of knowledge, I have learned that you can guard your faith through:

1. Associate with people who have the faith as yourself.
2. Put God first in your life and faith will work for you.
3. Embrace and know the value of faith.
4. Read, explore and develop your faith.
5. Live your life based on faith, not what you see.

What People Do with Faith

It was Tuesday evening, and I was walking on the shores of the Indian Ocean with a friend from Zimbabwe, Peter Gucu. We were discussing the question of beliefs or faith. My friend said that in matters of God, everyone knows and there is no authority about faith. He said anyone could interpret the scriptures. We never reached a standard position on several issues about faith. When I entered my hotel room, I had many ideas flowing on the subject. It coincided with the fact that I was writing a chapter about faith. The concept of faith is complicated, but here are some points to remember:

---

25   Mark 11: 22

1. Some people keep their faith. Never accept to lose it.
2. Some people fight with those of faith. Some people fight those who believe.
3. Some people ignore faith matters, no concern at all.
4. Some people discount faith or simply trash it.
5. Some people explore faith matters. Learn more about the topic of faith.
6. Some people neglect the faith issues, never bother with it.
7. Some people deepen their faith and seek to know more.
8. Some people misunderstand or confuse issues of faith.

Nobody can explain the mysteries of life. Some things have defied and defeated human knowledge and wisdom. The only way to understand the mysteries of life is by believing.

Chapter 7

FAMILY

You don't choose your family.
They are God's gift to you, as you are to them.
— ***Desmond Tutu***

The Value Of A Family: Hope And Stability

How does a family make a significant difference in the life of individuals? What impact does it have at a personal level or even national? In the early 2000s, I was in Soroti in Eastern Uganda where I was working at the time with World Vision. I got information about the death of one notorious robber, rebel and former soldier who had terrorized our village for years. For the sake of privacy, I will refer to that family using the name, "Dodes." I also knew other brothers of that rebel who was our neighbors in my rural birthplace. The brothers almost had the same behavior or traits. They all always had criminal tendencies and behavior. They had been in jail several times. I asked about these family members. They were known for burglary, murder, theft of cattle and conflict over land. I received a message recently that the surviving brother—our neighbor—has again crossed the land boundaries and our family is going to open a case with the local council.

When I trace the lineage of the Dodes, their great grandfather, born in 1910, had same behaviors. I was told that the grandfather was a heavy drinker, hated work, liked eating meat but also liked grabbing or stealing people's property. When I visited our village years back, I had an opportunity to meet most of the people in the local church. In our local church, the priests or church leaders will ask those who have been away for a long time to greet people. I always have that kind of opportunity. In crowds among the church congregations, I was able to see people I had never seen in so many years, including the relatives of the rebel I mentioned previously.

After the Sunday church service, I asked about my cousin whose home was near the Dodes. My cousin said that family is responsible for producing paupers, criminals, thieves, fighters and harlots. I felt so bad because the image of the family is so bad that any mention of that name scares people away. Are such people born with genes for bad behavior? The answer is no. Everybody is born innocent, but their character that becomes their destiny is shaped by family values and their environment. If you think about the Dodes family, there is one thing that you might see: The Dodes family is negatively perceived. The impact on generations is horrible. The descendants of the Dodes are among the feared people in our community.

Another Family Different Than the Dodes

Again, for privacy, I will refer to this family as the "Duttuses." This family is also from the same community and only separated by a swamp. The distance between the Dodes and Duttuses is about 3-4 kilometers. The Duttuses had a different lifestyle and history. The old Duttus man was murdered during the war when he was of advanced age about 80. This man, however, was a respected church leader, had attended elementary school, was baptized and converted into a Catholic Christian. He had one wife and was a devoted family man. I was told that he had 12 children: five boys and seven girls. They are believed to have been married for about 54 years.

In 2014, when I was Soroti, I met one of the grandsons who became an engineer in one of the districts of Teso Sub-Region in Uganda. I asked him about where their brothers and sisters were, what they were doing career-wise and generally getting updated. I was prompted to ask because each time I drive passed the Duttus family, I often see changes, improvements, new buildings, structures, shops and some good houses constructed. As a matter of fact, over four homes from that Duttus family have well-painted homes in the village. I have always admired that community. The engineer was kind to speak to me and I learned a lot of what had happened ever since the death of the old man. I found that family had produced different kinds of professionals and role models; some of the grandchildren are now living in different countries such as Kenya, South Africa and the United Kingdom. The engineer said their family has managed to produce teachers, engineer, lawyers, businessmen, public servants and local leaders who are helping resolve community disputes.

What is the contrast? The pattern is easy to see or recognize. In math, we say it is easiest to deduce. A good family is important in life. It matters a lot. You might think this is a simple matter. Let me shock you. There are families where people are torn apart or brought down. There are families where people are built up. You need to study your family tree and see what traits are there. If there is something you don't like about it, try to change it or never do it. For instance, the first Dode grandfather was known for laziness, heavy drinking, etc. This might have been the cause. That you can change. But, there are things you can't change. Examples are your past, your ancestry, upbringing, background or how you have been treated. You might not change much, but you have the capacity to influence your descendants.

How?

You can choose to teach your descendants to be responsible, respectful, prayerful, hardworking, honest, trustworthy and serve as role models. All these are what is known as fundamental values and principles. Why must values be taught? It is simple: Values and principles never change. Principles and values are universal. They are constant. Anywhere in the world, people want people who are honest, disciplined, faithful and so forth. There are many things you can do and things you cannot do. You can decide to work on things or neglect them. You decide to live with toxic or nontoxic relatives. The way the Duttus and Dodes families came into existence was due to lifestyle and decisions of an earlier generation or family leaders. A family has a profound effect on life, legacy and progress. I know another family like the Duttuses with similar results—accountants, engineers, businessman, pastors, policemen, teachers, politicians and other responsible persons. Difficult families produce difficult people at times. So, one goal in life must be working to make a family soft to ensure stability and strength. A good family is like an insurance company. It is like a safety net. It is like a haven in the storm. It is like a shade when there is too much sunshine. It is like an umbrella when it is raining. Strive to create a good family.

Is Your Home a Safe Haven or Hell?

In Kampala, Nairobi and most cities in which I have lived, I found that most people go to work early morning and use the same opportunity to take kids to school. The day starts at 5 AM by getting children ready to go to school, bathing, making tea, giving breakfast, dressing and then running to the car, off to school. Then, the husband takes the wife to work and proceeds to his office. The office demands result. The bills are not cleared. There are outstanding loans. Then by afternoon, there is an emergency from an upcountry relative asking for assistance. By 4:30 PM, the husband must go to pick up the kids who must be picked up by 5:30 PM. Any delays there will result in a school penalty. On the way to school, roads are open and traffic is flowing. But, arriving at school, almost all parents are rushing to pick up their kids. As they exit the school, traffic has built up, resulting in traffic jams. The wife is calling the husband to be picked from her place of work. Finally, they join and head back home. By now, it is 7 PM. Kids take a shower, do their homework, and by 9:30 PM, they go to bed. This routine is repeated for years.

In addition, the parents are struggling to make ends meet and helping dependent relatives. Question: What do you think is going on in the minds of the husbands and wives? Is there peace or chaos, stress or . . . if this goes on for years—say 15 years because the parents have four kids separate by just a few years. What do you expect? In such a situation, what kind of home do you want—a safe haven or hell. That is what is happening, and that is why most families are breaking up. Life is just not easy. So, having a stable family will save a lot. There are lessons to learn from these stories, and I believe life is just about stories.

Why A Family Is Significant

A Sanctuary and Haven for Peace

As I have pointed previously, families are grappling with challenges or pressures daily. The demands come from places of work where some of the supervisors or managers treat their employees as objects. Also, the impact of technology and information has made the pace of life uncontrollable. All big cities such as Lagos, Nairobi, Kampala, Dar es Salaam, Bombay, New Delhi, Cairo and many others have traffic challenges. Driving from one place to another is a nightmare. Unemployment, poverty, diseases, health-related and other crises all impact people. Where does a person find peace amid such storms, chaos, challenges and stress? The only place is in their families or homes. But, some families are also a nightmare. For some families, conflict and tension among parents are the order of the day. The only way to have peace in a family is to set up rules and laws observed by everyone. Family values also must also be agreed upon and lived by at times. Values and principles of life are transplanted when children are young. As they grow, they model those principles and values. For me, my benefits have protected me from many different problems.

A Foundation for Success and Development

When I think through the impact families have on their children, I believe that anything good comes from a foundation. Successful marriages are not often accidents; they come from good examples. If parents are successful in their marriage or relationship, the chances are high that even children will have the same behavior and values impacted. King Solomon said, "Start children off on the way they should go, and even when they are old they will not turn from it."26 When a child receives training at an early age, they will never depart from that knowledge or values. A strong foundation can withstand all storms. Thus, strong families operate similarly.

A Family Determines the Character of a Person

Our world has two types of people: those with good character or those with evil character. We have people are honest or dishonest. We have hardworking or lazy people. We have disciplined or undisciplined people. We have responsible or irresponsible adults. How does this happen? These

---

26   Proverbs 22:6.

characteristics start from a family. I grew up in a Christian family where going to Sunday school was a must and non-negotiable. I was taught about God, having faith and trusting in God. I was also informed about fundamental values. Those values have been part of my character. I have also continued to transfer those values to my children and I hope they will do the same for their children. Those values (listed in Chapter 15) have protected me; you can check them out.

Further, a person's character is modeled from the early or formative years and usually difficult to change. As children grow, their role is also shaped. Aggressive people, for instance, learn aggressiveness from childhood. I recall my experience when I made a mistake to steal pounded groundnuts from my grandmother's cupboard when I was nine. My grandmother was seated with my mother near a tree. They called and asked me when they saw I was eating something. I remember trying to pretend or cover up, but they asked me where I had gotten what I was eating. I started to avoid their questions; then my mother got hard or hot on me. She became tough and started to pinch me and beat me up; then, I confessed my mistake (sin). Then she told me never to do it again and warned me that if I continued, I would be staying in jail in future. Since that lesson on that day, I have avoided all the temptations to steal or lie about things. I remember my father was also a strict disciplinarian. He always said, "Tell the truth always." That teaching has stayed with me until now, and I will never depart from it. The character is a collection of all values and beliefs that have been adopted over the years. Attitude determines your destiny in life. If you have a good character, it will take you higher and keep you there.

A Family as a Place of Unconditional Love

A family where conditions are attached to love is not a good one. If chaos, confusion or hostility exists in a home, then it is not the best set up for children. That environment causes children or even adults to have low self-esteem, self-confidence and self-worth. There should be forgiveness and unconditional love even if people make mistakes, errors or do bad things. There must be patience and tolerance. My parents, uncles and aunts always loved me. This impacted me in my life to love people. The environment also helped me to learn and it made me know myself. The greatest challenge of life is knowing thy self. Most people never discover themselves because of their environment. However, some people come from difficult backgrounds or families. Paul wrote,

> *Not that I have already obtained all this, or have already arrived at my goal, but I press on to take hold of that for which Christ Jesus took hold of me. Brothers and sisters, I do not consider myself yet to have taken hold of it. But one thing I do: Forgetting what is behind and straining toward what is ahead, I press on toward the goal to win the prize for which God has called me heavenward in Christ Jesus.*[27]

This teaching from Paul has protected me from past experiences in life. I believe people must come to terms with any past if they had difficult history or relationships. You might have had a bad relationship with your parents; you must forget and forgive, so you do not become a victim of the past and repeat some of those patterns of behaviors. The most important relationship you must protect is those with your immediate family. Mother Teresa said, "If you judge people, you have no time to love them."[28] In most families, you will find a habit where people are torn apart by other members. You will never feel loved if others always judge you. That person is just not the same. Each person is different and unique.

---

27 Philippians 3:12-14

28 https://www.psychologytoday.com/us/blog/the-gift-maybe/201504/if-you-judge-people-you-have-no-time-love-them

Making The Commitment To Care For My Family

I grew up with my grandparents and my parents. In those years, I could observe how my grandfather treated my grandmother. I also watched how they lived their lives. However, one thing that I never saw was quarreling. I never found fights. I grew up with that notion of a family. When got my own family, I decided that I want to minimize as much as possible to avoid conflicts. Here is my advice to those reading this book about what you need to do.

1. **Choose your priorities.** For me, the most important things in life are God, my family, my purpose and friends. I care about family. I try to protect and provide for them. If you do not have a family, then you are poorer. Mother Teresa also said, "The most terrible poverty is loneliness and the feeling of being unloved."[29] A family should be given top priority if a stable relationship and foundation are to be established. A healthy family is built and requires hard work.

2. **Establish family rules.** My spouse is a strict enforcer of rules and regulations regarding our family. Those rules have guided us concerning setting the direction of the family. Those rules come from values that we decided on as a family. I have seen whenever we find lousy behavior, we return to our laws then to correct that.

3. **Learn how to solve problems.** One of the strategies or philosophies and principle that has helped in solving problems is dialogue and knowledge that everything has a season. Issues are the cause of major conflicts in most families. If couples do not have a better strategy for solving issues, then it can affect the family.

---

29 https://scholarscompass.vcu.edu/cgi/viewcontent.cgi?article=1016&context=vcoa_editorial

4. **Put your family as a top priority.** Let your family be an asset and top priority. Have fun time, one-on-one time and always be together.

5. **Celebrate family events and traditions.** Celebrating events such as women days, birthdays and public holidays. These days must be used for bonding. Visit your relatives and friends. Keep memories, pictures and albums.

6. **Spend time together as possible.** Life is too short. You never know when you will be no more. Always learn to spend time with your loved ones. I often regret the short time I spent with my mother who passed on when I was 14.

7. **Appreciate the contributions of each other.** The use of the words such as "Thank you" or "sorry" are not typical of most families. Every person wants to be appreciated. People should start receiving appreciation and affirmation from their home before they can look for it from outside. The world sometimes does not give affirmation or gratitude. I try to appreciate my family and kids. I keep building them up and affirming them. I have seen that each time I send a message or tell them something positive, their confidence goes up.

8. **Find ways to resolve conflicts.** No family is immune to conflicts. All marriages have challenges that must be managed. A family's capacity to solve problems can either develop or destroy it. Never ignore any issues that can affect the family. Be there for each and support one another. Some people cannot cope with pressures of life. Some are resilient. I think I am one person who is resilient with a never-give-up attitude.

9. **Communicate openly to each other.** I have a confession to make: I often have a weakness in communication. Communication is critical in building relationships. Always try to share freely and openly with your family. Avoid hiding things from each other.

Chapter 8

GOALS

A goal without a plan is just a wish.
— Antoine de Saint-Exupery

From Ideas To Goals And Results

After you have developed your ideas, what should you do next? To me, there are a series of steps that must be undertaken.

- Start to capture those ideas so that you can turn them into great goals.
- Become self-disciplined so that action is taken.
- Stop procrastination and no time should be allowed to be lost.
- Always act when the ideas have been received to avoid losing the idea.
- Being sincerely disciplined requires that you develop the ability to act. You don't need to be too hasty, but you also don't want to lose much time. The time to act is when the idea strikes us—when it is hot—and the emotion is strong before the feeling passes and the

idea dies. If you don't, you'll fall prey to the law of diminishing intent. A month from today, the passion will be cold. A year from now, it won't be located or found.

- So, act now.

For every disciplined effort, there are multiple rewards or benefits. You never get a reward unless you have done something. That is how life is arranged. If you sow well or abundantly, you will reap well or abundantly. Have you seen a farmer sow a basin of beans; what did they get afterward? They get more. Life on Earth is built on laws that both govern and explain behaviors. The ancient laws of sowing and reaping might well be the significant law we need to understand: For every disciplined effort, there are multiple rewards or benefits

How Do You Set Goals?

This is an area most people find to be very challenging. Personally, I have seen people have limited capacity to set personal goals. In this section, I will show you how to set goals. There is a process of doing it. Life always has choices. Choices are made based on the alternatives. Every person has decisions to make, either to live or design a life he or she want. They can plan or not plan for whatever they want in life. We either make a living, or we can design a life. Preparing or developing a life requires the setting of goals. The most critical benefit for goal setting is not the achievement of the goal itself. Instead, it's what you do and the person you become to achieve your goal that are the real benefits.

To help you with these processes, here are some key questions to ask yourself:

- What do I want to do?
- What do I want to have?
- Where do I want to go?
- What contribution do I want to make in the world?
- What do I want to learn?
- Who do I want to meet and spend my time with?
- How much do I want to earn, save and invest?
- What kind of life do I want to live?

Principles For Setting Your Greatest Goals

First, goal setting is an essential obligation that gives focus and thus shapes dreams. Goals provide direction and guide on actions required to be performed to achieve everything that life desires. Goals need to be set high because they cause us to stretch and grow in ways that we never have before. To reach our goals, we must become better.

Secondly, life is designed in such a way that we look long-term but live short-term, in the now or present. God gives every human a day at a time, so we do not live all the days in one moment. God gave each person a day, so we can live long enough in our dreams and enjoy the benefits of the dream and fulfil our vision. Everyone dreams of a better future but must live in the present or moment. Unfortunately, the present can produce many difficult obstacles, challenges, and problems. Most people live according to what they see every day. They never have a vision for their future. But setting goals provides long-term vision in our lives and makes life exciting. we all need important or long-range goals to help get us past those short-term problems or obstacles. Fortunately, the more powerful the goals are, the more you are willing to act on them, which will help guarantee success and results.

Steps To Goal Setting

1. **Evaluate, Reflect and Review.** Knowing where you are right now and knowing your current level of satisfaction are the only ways you can reasonably determine what you want in the future as well as how you can get there. The starting point is taking some time (that is, days, weeks and so forth) to think thoroughly. Write down your current situation; then ask this question on each key point: Is that okay? You need to carry out a self-assessment. In my book, *Strategic Planning: Understanding The 3Ps — Power, Purpose, and Process,* I have described in greater details about the process and methods for carrying out the evaluation. I have also explained the tangible rewards of applying evaluation. In this book, the purpose of the evaluation is twofold. First, it gives you an objective way to look at your accomplishments, current strengths, and weaknesses as you pursue the vision you have for life. Secondly, it shows you where you are (or baseline), so you can determine where you need to go or destination (or target). Evaluation enables you to have a baseline from which to work. You will be able to know what needs to be done and what does not need to be done.

Where to start? I will recommend that you take time (maybe a week) to evaluate, review and reflect. See where you are and write it down so that as the month's progress or years and you continue a regular time of evaluation and reflection, you will see just how much ground you're gaining—and that will be exciting! It will motivate you.

2. **Define the dreams and goals you want to achieve.** One of the amazing things we have been given as humans is the unquenchable desire to have dreams of a better life. We have the ability and capacity to establish and set goals to live out those dreams. We

can look deep into our hearts, passions and desires. We dream of a better situation for ourselves and our families. We can dream of better economic, political, legal, environmental, social, financial, emotional, spiritual or physical lives. We can dream of better life for kids, families or communities. We have also been endowed with the ability to not only dream, but also pursue those dreams. We can take it even further. We not only can pursue our dreams, but we also have the cognitive ability to lay out a plan and strategies to achieve them. Everyone dreams, but the problem is many of us never pursue our dreams. To achieve anything, you need to master some principles. I have a few principles that I have applied all my life. They are documented in my book, *Success Principles: Proven Secrets for Achieving Your Dreams and Vision.*

What Are Your Goals or Dreams? This is not about what you have already done or what you have, but rather about what you desire or want. Have you ever really sat down, meditated and thought through your life values? Did you decide what you truly want? Have you ever taken the time off to reflect, to listen quietly to your heart and to see what dreams live inside you or within you? Your dreams are there. Everyone has them. They might live right on the surface, or they might be buried deep from years of others telling you that you cannot achieve those dreams. Some of your dreams have been destroyed by your environment or culture. Sometimes your parents, friends or teachers have told you, be realistic. You cannot achieve those dreams. But the writer of this book also experienced the same challenges. I confess that I was told many times of things I dreamt that could not happen. For instance, I was told I cannot complete a doctorate. I was told ideas about a school or leadership center were unrealistic. I decided to ignore and write my dreams down. I wrote my goals down and I believed my goals. Every day I would keep checking on my dreams or goals. As I write, those goals have been achieved, or they are somewhere under implementation.

I would recommend that you take time off to be quiet or silent. This is one thing that most people don't do enough of in this busy, chaotic and complex world that we live. People rush, rush, rush without sitting down to reflect or meditate. Very many people listen to every noise that occurs in our surroundings. The human heart was meant to have times of quietness—to see inside of the heart. It is when we do this that our hearts are set free to soar and take flight on the wings of our dreams. Schedule some quiet "dream time" this week or in the coming months. During the dream week or months, there should be no other people—no smartphone, no computer. Just you, a pad, a pen, a book and your thoughts. Let the thoughts fly and take careful record.

In my own experience, I have applied these steps to my planning process. I recall I used to go to quiet places by myself and sit alone. Afterward, spending time (like two hours), then I know what I am supposed to be doing exactly for the next few months. When I worked outside of the home in other parts of the world like Somalia, Kenya, Nigeria and so forth, I got opportunities to be alone in a quiet room. The whole night was about dreaming and writing down the plans. It was during those moments that I came to conclude my reason for living on Earth.

Think about what thrills or inspires you. When you are quiet, think about those things that get your blood moving, captivate your deepest desires. What are the things you would do if you had only six months to live? What things would make you enjoy or have fun for a living? What would you like to accomplish? What would you try if you were guaranteed to succeed? What big thoughts move your heart into a state of excitement and joy?

When you answer these questions, you will feel great; you will be in the "dream zone." It is only when we get to this point that we experience what our dreams are. Write down all your dreams as you have them. Just allow your mind to process your thoughts and take careful record.

The next process is to prioritize the dreams or thoughts. Which ones are the most important? Which are the most feasible or achievable? Which of the many ideas would you love to do for the rest of your life?

3. **Ensure Your Goals are S.M.A.R.T.** The acronym S.M.A.R.T. means Specific, Measurable, Attainable, Realistic and Time-sensitive.

   - **Specific:** Goals are no place to waffle. They are no place to be vague. Ambiguous goals produce ambiguous results. Incomplete goals produce incomplete futures. Poor goals produce poor results. Goals must be as specific as possible. You need to document precisely what you want.

   - **Measurable:** Always set goals that are measurable. I would say "specifically measurable" considering our principle of being specific.

   - **Attainable:** One of the harmful problems that many people do—with good intentions—is setting goals that are so high and unattainable or unreachable.

- **Realistic:** The root or foundation word for realistic is "real." A goal is a desire, passion or idea that is "real" or gives a "reality" in life. There are some goals that people set that are merely not real or realistic. You must be able to say—even if it is a tremendously stretching goal—that without a doubt it is entirely realistic, that you could or should make it. You might also have to say that if I do A, B, and C to complete it and after all my energies have been exhausted—if those happen, then it could be achieved or done. The point is about being realistic.

- **Time-bound:** Every goal should have a timeframe attached, set and connected to it. One of the compelling aspects and characteristics of a high goal is that it has an end. It has a timeline when you accomplish it or finish activity implementation to create the desired results. As time passes, you keep working on it and you don't want to get behind or fail to get it done. The activities and work are completed with diligence to beat the deadline. Sometimes, a big goal is broken down into smaller parts of measurement and timeframes. Breaking the goal down makes it manageable and doable. Also, set smaller goals and work them out in their own time. A S.M.A.R.T. goal has a timeline or a deadline. For instance, if your goal is to write a book, decide the chapters and set a deadline for each chapter when you must have it completed. If you have a goal to complete a degree at college, set a deadline when it must be completed. You can set a goal for any of your dreams.

- **Hold yourself accountable:** When someone knows what the goals you have set for yourself, then they have the responsibility to hold you accountable. They demand that you "give an account" of where you are in the process of achieving that goal. Suppose a goal has been set and only one person or few people know of it, does it have any power? Many times, they do not. A goal isn't as powerful if you don't have one or more people who can hold you accountable to it.

The Significance of Setting Goals

I am going to start this section with rhetorical questions. No answers needed. A person without goals will always be living below their potential. What people achieve is directly related to the goals set then in the past. The first action in goal setting is to write the goals down. One way to start is writing down 101 things you do before you die. Set a date against each of the things you want to do. You can jot down your thoughts if you wish. Why are goals important? What do goals do? What do goals create? Why do some people set goals? Why do some people fear to set goals? One of the general reasons for goal setting is because some people have a burning desire to achieve those goals.

However, the primary reason for setting goals is not what you will gain or achieve, but what it will make you become. Goals make you a different person. For example, I remember when I set a goal to pursue a doctorate. Goals made me gain writing, research and presentation skills that I did not have. I remember when I set a goal to establish a local project; that goal made become influential and a leader. I also recall the goal of writing a book. That goal made me become an author and writer. Do you see the benefits?

Why Goals Matter To Me

There are many reasons why goals matter to me and you too can decide your reason.

- Goals make those with goals great. People without goals aim at nothing. They never have anything that makes them motivated.
- Goals are a source of motivation and pull you through problems.
- Goals give direction. Where you end up in life is determined by your goals and what you do daily. Your daily plan and agenda are created by goals. Goals are the road maps that provide guidance of the desired destination.
- Goals are a source of self-discipline. Without goals, there is no self-control. But with goals, you know what to do and what not to do.
- Goals give people focus.
- Goals cause you to become resilient.
- Goals make you stronger or weaker.
- Goals give you hope for a better tomorrow or future.
- Goals give you the opportunity to learn.
- Goals enable you to release your potential.
- Goals remind you of your obligations and responsibility.
- Goals hold you accountable.
- Goals give you a roadmap and guide your course of action.
- Goals create activities or actions.
- Goals help in resource mobilization.
- Goals protect you from doing wrong things and help you focus on right things.
- Goals create opportunities for relationships.
- Goals have power.
- Goals cause changes and transformation.
- Goals make the mind more aware of what needs to be accomplished.

Ten Tips For Setting Your Personal And Greatest Goals

I want you to remember that the concept of "goals" can be intimidating or frightening or scary. It can feel so overbearing that it keeps people from even beginning the process. Through several years of experience and working with various organizations, I got a discovery whereby goals are a to-do list with deadlines or specific timeframes. Do the goals have deadlines? When do you hope to achieve or accomplish? Tomorrow, next week, several months or next year or five years' time? Goals with a short-term period (that is, two, three, five, or more years) are short-term goals. Life goals are a to-do list for the rest of your life. Goals can be added, subtracted and, most important, scratched off or removed from the list as you move through your life. (If you want to learn more on goal setting, you can access another resource, *Strategic Planning: Understanding the 3 P's—The Power, Purpose and Process*).

Meanwhile, here are some things to remember about goals:

1. **Goals must be personal.** Goals make meaning when they are for you. That is, not for your spouse, your children or your employer. But rather, yours. If you allow other people to determine the way you define success, you're sabotaging your future. When you do not have your personal goals, I think you are in trouble. You are likely to face problems. Goals help you have a plan. If you have a game plan, then you know what you are expected to accomplish.

2. **Goals must mean something to you personally.** When you write down the goals, you must also ask yourself, "What's important to me? What am I prepared to give up making this happen and occur?" Write also the reasons for charting a new course of action or direction. When you write reasons, they give you the drive and energy to get up every morning. Goals cause you to think and reflect.

3. **Goals must be specific and measurable.** Vague generalizations and wishful statements aren't good enough. Be specific. Can you measure your goals? Can you count? For instance, how many books do you intend to write in a year? Is it two or four? How many books do you want to read per month?

4. **Goals must be flexible.** A flexible plan keeps you from feeling suffocated and allows you to take advantage of genuine opportunities that walk in your future door. Goals should give you breathing space. You need to get time to rest.

5. **Goals must be challenging, exciting and inspiring.** Force yourself to jump out or leap out of the comfort zone to acquire that energy and edge. Challenging goals cause you to move out of comfort zone to a challenging environment.

6. **Goals must be aligned with your personal or core values.** You need to pay special attention to intuition and instinct. Whenever you set a goal that contradicts your values, something inside is a miss. You must pay attention to your values. Values should never be changed, but goals can be reviewed.

7. **Goals must be well-balanced.** Make sure you include areas that allow time to relax, have fun and enjoy people in your closest circle.

8. **Goals must be realistic.** Set a goal that you can do or reach.

9. **Goals must include a contribution.** What contribution will your goal bring to others? Goals should contribute or bring benefit to others. Goals should give meaning to life.

10. Goals need to be supported. You can choose to share the ideas, dreams, desires, passions or vision with a few selected people. In any case, you must create a web of support as well as accountability for yourself. Plan to have some quiet time. Write down 101 goals. Open your mind to all the possibilities. You need to start each goal with "I am" or "I will." Don't even think about restricting yourself.

Apply Focus And Discipline To Achieve Goals

Let me begin with this statement: If you do a good job, your rewards shall be multiplied or increased. If you're fair, honest, consistent and patient with others, then your rewards will be automatically multiplied. If you give more then you expect to receive, you may earn more rewards. However, remember, the key words here—as you might well imagine—are focus and discipline.

Everything of value requires care, attention and discipline. Our thoughts need focus and discipline. We must consistently and persistently determine the inner boundaries, or our thoughts or ideas become confused. Moreover, if our thoughts or ideas are confused, it merely implies we will become hopeless. If you have confused thoughts, then you will produce chaotic outcomes or results.

Remember the law: For every disciplined effort, there will be multiple rewards or benefits. Learn the discipline of writing a card or a letter to a friend. Learn the discipline of paying your bills on time or arriving at appointments on time or using your time more effectively. Learn the discipline of paying attention, paying your bills, paying taxes or paying yourself. Learn the discipline of having regular meetings and interactions with your friends, colleagues, associates, your spouse, your child or your parents. You need to learn the discipline of learning everything you can learn; teaching everything you can teach; or reading everything you can read. Also, learn the discipline of working hard.

Focus on your goals, not of anything that scares or frightens you. Most people never act on their ideas because of fear. Instead, they focus on fear instead of their goals. My simple advice is always focus on the goals set instead of focusing on your fears.

><><><><><><><><><><><><><><><><><><><><><><><><><><><><><><><><><><><><><><>

*Always focus on the goals set
instead of focusing on your fears.*

><><><><><><><><><><><><><><><><><><><><><><><><><><><><><><><><><><><><><><>

How do you focus? When you are focused on your goals, then you will achieve your goals. Staying focused is always a difficult thing for most people as they get distractions. People are distracted by setbacks, past experiences, problems and challenges, including defeats or failures. Every time you stay focused, then your goals become reachable. Those who focus on their goals always grow; however, those who get distracted never grow. Suppose your goals have not been attained. Does it mean you are a failure? The answer is no. Failure is part of the process for any success.

Another way to look at success is to consider failure as the stairs that you keep climbing until you finally reach your goal. That goal becomes your success. You will never be successful in life without setbacks, problems, challenges and defeats. For instance, each time you solve a problem, another problem appears. I hope you can see this as I see it. For example, when you buy a vehicle for personal transport, other problems start to emerge such maintaining and fueling the car. If you have been unemployed, employment can become another problem because it might separate you from being near your loved ones. You can also examine or see failure as a teacher.

Furthermore, lessons should be taken when you fail. Learn from every failure, but keep on moving towards the goal, keep climbing the stairs or the mountain, until you arrive at the peak. Failure is a bend in the road of life but is not the end of the road. I have seen people who failed and bounced back. Success in life does not mean the complete absence of problems, but instead, success is your ability to bounce back after failure and overcoming obstacles.

Chapter 9

GROWTH

Growth is the great separator between those who succeed and those who do not. When I see a person beginning to separate themselves from the pack, it's almost always due to personal growth. – **John C. Maxwell.**

Learning After Formal Education

When I started writing this chapter, I reflected on a couple of friends with whom I completed college and several of them with whom I attended primary school. I had three questions: What happened to them? Did they manage to exploit opportunities for growth? What were the results of their growth efforts and initiatives? I noticed that some people were fortunate to continue for their master's; others went into business; and others got jobs. In my case, I remember my own experiences after my first-degree course from Makerere University; I was unable to go back for further studies for about six years. There were many obstacles. I worked at the time; my spouse had gone for first degree; and my siblings were in high school and university. I also had cousins to look after as well as care for my parents and other relatives. In Africa, I am referring to the issue of extended family. I was the only person who had a formal job. The responsibilities and obligations were overwhelming to me, only one person.

Another issue was that my income was meager and there were insufficient opportunities to generate additional income to cover the living costs. Sometimes, I lived on very low or tight budget. These two important factors significantly hampered my ability to advance my informal education. There were no chances of going back to school. If I were to further my studies, I was responsible to pay the costs of advancing my education. I was fortunate to have completed my first degree through a government scholarship.

During the time I was not at university; I noticed I was not growing in my career. I was mentally stagnant and had no new ideas. I did not depend and rely on my work experiences and few learning opportunities my employers offered me. Anything that I learned during this time was like chance or luck. I say luck because managers or leaders made the decision for me to attend workshops, seminars, meetings or trainings. Some decisions were made in my favor while others were entirely against me. In those moments, my ideas were starving because of relying on old or outdated information.

The Concept Of Lifelong Learning

Do you realize that when people complete their formal education, they pursue careers, marriages and wealth? I have noticed most people stop seeking educational opportunities after they graduate. They get jobs and then start living their lives without any hustle. They watch television after working, listen to the news or watch sports. In my experiences, I have concluded that formal education will enable you to earn daily bread or a living. Most people never realize that a significant portion of life is lived on Earth after formal education. That means years after formal education tend to be more profitable in comparison to the years of formal education. Moreover, people will have mastered what is required to live a successful life.

One of the phases and goals I wrote in my journals was "to be a lifelong learner." To be ahead in life, you must become a lifelong learner. I learned everything I know even though I was born with natural intelligence or talents. Most people do not have that concept of being a lifelong learner engraved in their hearts. I believe a successful life is usually the one with a lifelong learning attitude and commitment. To put it another way, a successful person is a lifelong learner and planner.

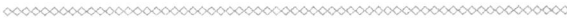

A successful person is a lifelong learner and planner.

The Power of Self-Education Over Formal Education

To me, self-education is more potent than formal education. Some people who have formal education may behave as if they have never been to college because they are shallow and mediocre. You will realize that they do not know most of the things required for a successful life. Do you know anyone whose formal education has not benefited them? How many of your graduated classmates from college know everything that they need in life? I believe that most of the educated people who have completed college or school might never know what is required to succeed in life. For instance, some complete a medical degree but do not have managerial, supervisory or business skills. This person is not likely to be a competent manager. The point is that if you want to excel and succeed, then you need both formal and self-education. Sometimes, your parents or guardians force you to complete formal education, but self-education is more voluntary and a personal initiative. If formal education is not sufficient, then self-education plays a significant role in the life of an individual. Therefore, self-education is a key to opportunities.

Learning is the beginning
of everything in life.

When a child is born, they learn a language; they learn to communicate. Everything that I learned, I first learned from my parents, grandparents, uncles and aunties, friends, teachers and professors. I also learned through experiences, books, reading, watching, observing and reflection. I learned all that I know. Learning has helped me earn everything I have needed in life. The following are some additional thoughts about learning:

- Wealth begins when you learn.
- Health begins when you learn.
- Knowledge starts when you learn.

- Spiritual growth occurs when you learn.
- Productivity starts when you learn.
- Growth begins when you learn
- Improvements start when you learn.
- Change starts when you learn.

Alternatively, we could "flip" these sayings around to include the following:

- Learning is the beginning of wealth.
- Learning is the beginning of health.
- Learning is the beginning of knowledge.
- Learning is the beginning of development.
- Learning is the beginning of productivity.
- Learning is the beginning of growth.
- Learning is the beginning of improvements.
- Learning is the beginning of change.

In order to learn, you must be willing to search for knowledge. When you search, you will discover and know. Most people never take time to search for knowledge. They walk around with old knowledge and outdated information. They also depend heavily on life experiences. I always have thoughts about life. How many years are spent in school? How many years are spent on a formal education? The answers to these questions might vary but imagine the big question: How many years are spent on Earth after formal education? If you figure out the answers to these questions, you will realize that successful persons are those who chose and decide to make learning a priority for their entire lives.

How To Improvements And Change

Often, I have been asked the following questions: How can I improve and change my life? How can I make myself better? My initial thoughts include: If you want to improve, then you must improve; if you want to change, then you must change; and if you want to become better, then you must become better. Is that difficult? To improve, change and become better, you need self-education. Some people would call it personal development. You see in both answers something to do with yourself – self or personal.

The other strategies for self-education or personal development include:

1. **Engaging in the serious reading of books related to your area of interest.** You pursue this until you become an expert.

2. **Observing others.** This is helpful in gaining insights into what makes other people successful or failures. There are always two categories of people: successful and unsuccessful ones.

3. **Self-reflecting.** It is essential to reflect on your experiences in life continually. You will be able to notice what went well or what did not.

In my own life, I have learned that most problems have solutions in books, experiences and lessons from the lives of other people. Now let me say something about books. Books are costly to buy; they cost money. On average, I spend over $400 on books every month. Books are expensive, but books contain ideas. Ideas are the most potent force on Earth. Everything available on Earth including iPhones, smartphones, cars, airplanes, clothes, buildings, roads, houses or anything that you have owned or own were created and produced from ideas. How can you fail to buy a book? Yet, books contain concepts that have built wealth, health, growth, improvement or change.

Some people never buy books because they are costly or expensive. These same people purchase smartphones, purchase fast foods, buy expensive clothing, use costly perfumes, carry high-dollar bags, drive fancy cars, etc. Some people even go for holidays in the name of enjoying life after work or formal education. They imagine it is a waste of time and money to buy books. This is where I have a problem. If books are costly, have you estimated what it will cost you for not reading them? What about the knowledge you will miss as well?

The most important question to ask yourself is how much will it cost you if you do not read books. You might not realize the costs. Ignorance, however, is a dangerous enemy and a cause of poverty and disease among other factors. When a person decides to read, however, he or she becomes open to a vast view of the world; they begin to imagine possibilities, opportunities and ideas. They begin to understand things. If a person reads a book, that person will have new ideas; those ideas are like seeds. If seeds are planted in the soil, they will germinate and produce fruits. If ideas start to grow in minds and hearts, they produce fruits, accomplishments, results, achievements and successes.

Here is another serious question: How can you grow and expand if you lack consistency and pro-activeness in pursuing knowledge that help move your life forward? The answer to that question is not for me to give you or even guess. If you have been avoiding spending money on books, then you now understand why books matter.

- **Read books:** You now can change your mind and buy every book in the markets. You must also set goals for self-education or personal development. Mine is that I must read four books a month. My plans are higher; my dreams are higher. So, I need to cover a lot more ground.

- **Learn from the successful people:** You must also learn from people who are successful or unsuccessful. There is something good about learning from those who have failed. You will pick up critical lessons. Those lessons can change and improve your life. They can make your life better.

- **Learn from yourself:** You have made mistakes. Learn from them. You have enjoyed victories; learn what made you victorious.

Which Books To Read

This is a personal choice for everyone. My advice is to read the books connected to your dreams, passions and vision. If you are passionate about baking cakes, do not read books about becoming a pilot. If you are passionate about teaching, do not read books about politics. For me, my most magnificent book is the Bible. The Bible is an important book. It has life and success stories. It has stories of people who became successful as well as those who never made it. It also gives reasons for those who failed. You can learn from books.

Every person has potential.

The most significant discoveries I learned when I was a teenager was the concept of potential. I got this concept when God created the universe in Genesis 1 and 2. There are many verses in which potential is manifested. In my book, *Success Principles: Proven Secrets for Achieving Your Dreams and Vision*, I have written extensively on potential. Let me give you a practical example. In every mango seed, there is a tree and then mangoes, fruits, trees, etc. What makes every mango become a tree and then produce more fruits? It is because the potential that is inside a seed. The same is right about every person. Usually, our problem is we never know about our potential. If you want the seed to bring forth fruits, then you must grow the seed. Is this true? Yes. You cannot reveal the potential of a seed without growing the seed. This means that when you grow, your potential gets manifested. You get an increase in potential through growth. Growth is one way that gives you potential.

Let me share with you a personal experience. I worked with a dear colleague whose name is Joseph. We both had our first university degrees, but I was senior to him by one step, so I was assigned to supervise my friend Joseph directly. Watch what happened. After five months, Joseph went for his master's in Belgium. He resigned his position in the organization I was working and left me in the same position. When Joseph returned after 12 months, a higher position was advertised, and Joseph applied. He was appointed that job. I never got it! Joseph got the position because of growth and that gave him the potential for a higher position. That experience opened my eyes. I also enrolled for an advanced degree; guess what happened. I also grew and took over a more senior position. Growth is what gives you the potential in life.

Some Wrong Ideas About Growth

When I talk about wrong ideas, I am referring to misconceptions. When a person gets wrong ideas, it implies they have false concepts. It also means there is a misconception. When it comes to the subject of growth, here are some of the things I have learned over the years; I believe they are right.

1. **People think growth is automatic:** Most people misunderstand the process of growth. They think it occurs naturally, but this not true. Growth does not happen automatically. Growth occurs when there is a persistent effort. When we are children, there is natural growth that happens that is automatic for everyone. We start as infants, children, teenagers, adults and so forth. When starting school, we have our parents, teachers, religious leaders and other social networks that continue to motivate, inspire, challenge and force us to learn. Therefore, we mentally grow. But after school, the story changes. Perhaps, no other person is pushing to learn or improve. In that case, you likely stop growing. You could be significant in size but very small in knowledge or ideas.

   Personal growth is a personal responsibility. If you don't deliberately take full responsibility for your growth, it won't happen. Further, growth does not come because you are old. It is not your age that determines it; it is your effort. Personal growth does not grow as your bank account grows. It occurs when you keep depositing knowledge into your knowledge bank account.

2. **People think growth comes from information:** Today's world is full of too much information. Social media platforms are available in which information is transmitted faster than ever. You receive all sorts of ideas and messages. Some of these messages are truly inspirational and motivational. I believe that to grow, however, you need information. You don't need just any information. You need the right information and truth. When you comprehend the correct information, it becomes knowledge. If you can make better decisions out of that knowledge, then it useful knowledge and learning. Life changes when you have the right information, right understanding and proper application.

3. **People think growth comes from their experience:** There are many experienced leaders and workers all over the world. They have worked and gotten to higher positions. I want you to imagine the great football giants like Lionel Messi or Cristiano Ronaldo. Just think about these players only relying on their years of experience in football without training, commitment, dedication and practice. They would never grow unless they had those elements. Experience is a good thing, but it must be used to pick lessons and apply them.

Six Reasons Why Growth Counts Every Day

We have seen the misplaced views about growth. Now, that you have those points, let me also briefly summarize the six reasons that make growth very important. Think about each bullet point.

1. **Growth leads to effectiveness and efficiency:** If you want to be active and efficient, then you must keep growing. Every person has a gift that is buried; without watering, it will die. You could be born with a gift, but unless you keep nurturing and feeding it, it will not serve you. If you have a talent or a gift and you keep practicing (for instance, singing or playing the piano), it will help you.

2. **Growth increases your value or worth:** You remember the story of Joseph, who went back to school for his master's degree in Belgium? When Joseph returned and was offered another job, his value tripled compared to what he earned before his master's. Think about the greatly paid businessmen. How do they make money in the hotel industry? They grow their businesses through investments and adding value. Then, they earn more than the average business people.

3. **Growth reduces the chance of stagnation:** Every person wants to expand. They want to take on higher positions in companies. They want to be in charge. They want to lead and manage. If you're going to prevent stagnation, then you should continue growing. Some people get stuck in specific jobs and wonder what went wrong. The answer is simple. They stopped growing. I have seen people blame their circumstances, spouses, failures and other conditions as the causes for their stagnation. I disagree. To grow, you must make personal decisions, choices and internal changes. Growth should be one of your top goals because it helps reduce stagnation. Assume you have a mango seed that is not growing as expected; then, you need to study the soil where the seed is planted. Is it fertile ground? If not, then you need to do something different. For example, you might add nutrients, water and fertilizers.

4. **Growth causes improvement in your business:** To improve and grow your business, then you must have concrete plans for growth. Leaders must grow if the business is to grow. Otherwise, it will not be able to survive all the challenges that will come from external forces. The business environment is dynamic and changes rapidly. Unless there is internal growth, external survival and competition will be affected.

5. **Growth occurs through a commitment to continuous learning:** When I completed my doctorate, I thought I had learned everything I needed to take carry me through the maze of life. I was mistaken. I made a terrible mistake and paid the price for it. In one of those mistakes, I assumed if am committed, then those around me are also committed. I recall paying a hefty price of $5,000 for lack of commitment of one my employees. When I looked at the issue

deeply, I realized I should have fired the officer who was the leader and manager of my business. I never took the matter that way. I wanted to be a nice guy. In the end, I paid the price and I learned that I need to be committed all the time.

6. **Growth enables you to reach your potential:** Everyone has this treasure (potential), but most people never reach their potential. When you complete your first degree, that is no longer your potential. It means you have the potential to do something greater. If you finished writing a book, it implies you can write more books. However, if you do not grow, then your potential will not be reached.

What To Do About Personal Growth

I have a few points I want to emphasize for you about personal growth:

1. To grow personally, you need a personal growth or learning plan
2. To grow personally, you need to know your potential and tap into it.
3. To grow personally, you must have set goals.
4. To grow personally, you must commit to change and endure.
5. To grow personally, you must make personal choices and decisions.
6. To grow personally, you must estimate the costs and benefits.
7. To grow personally, you must set your own time for growth.
8. To grow personally, you must be motivated by your vision.
9. To grow personally, you must discipline yourself.
10. To grow personally, you must keep and apply what you have learned.

The Pillars for Sustaining Life

Chapter 10

HEALTH

Health is the greatest gift,
contentment the greatest wealth,
faithfulness the best relationship. —**Buddha**

The Linkage Of Dreams, Plans, Visions, And Health

Every person is born with a dream from the inside. They have desires and deep longings of things they want to accomplish and realize the meaning for life. They have inherent desire to rule, dominate and govern. They aspire to change the world. They have great ideas and visions for the future they want to see. These desires are inherent in God's creation, and God blessed them and said to them, "Be fruitful and increase in number; fill the earth and subdue it. Rule over the fish in the sea and the birds in the sky and over every living creature that moves on the ground."[30] How can you or anyone accomplish these obligations or responsibilities without good health?

---

30   Genesis 1: 28.

I remember a dear friend of mine who was terminally ill in 2013. This gentleman served as a public servant in the Ugandan government. He worked for over 20 years in public service. He had grand plans and was doing a lot of quick impact projects in his home district. The guy was very progressive and developmental, but his life was cut short by poor health. There were attempts to save his life, including seeking advanced medical assistance from India. A lot of friends tried to help and support him, but it was too late. He, unfortunately, lost the battle and his life ended. It was so sad, and today, all those ideas, plans and projects have remained incomplete or unattended.

I learned of another situation in which a gentleman was a founder of a hotel and petrol station near Busia in Eastern Uganda. I do not want to give details to protect the family. The guy was progressive; however, I am told he spent a lot of years drinking alcohol and living a reckless lifestyle. I understand he also smoked heavily. His lungs and general health were affected and eventually he passed away. There are also other cases of people whom I met in Mukono, Kampala, and Soroti who had similar practices: drinking alcohol, smoking and living wild lives. There are several examples of people all over the world like the examples I mentioned. I often wonder why someone would get to a level of doing things that can shorten their lives without stopping those practices and habits. Someone said to me years ago that habits die hard. There are good and bad habits. If you have good habits, they can protect your life. They are fundamental to achieving dreams, plans, visions and lifelong desires.

However, if the habits are wrong, then they also shorten life. How do you look at your health? Is it good or bad? I believe and agree with what Buddha said, "Health is the greatest gift, contentment the greatest wealth,

Health

faithfulness the best relationship." Your health is the best and most significant gift that you can have. Have you imagined what you can accomplish when you have good health? I believe you can achieve more. Think of people whom you know who had great potential but never did anything with their lives because they were bedridden or ill. In the early 1990s, I was a young boy living in in hospital quarters. There were nurses' quarters. Most of those nurses passed on in the late 1990s or early 2000s due to HIV/Aids. At that time, there were no drugs for HIV/Aids. Sometimes, I ask questions about what could have happened if they had lived healthily and reduced the risk of getting or acquiring HIV that causes AIDs.

Why Does Health Matter In Life?

You have possible answers to this question. But, I want to say something that helped and changed my life. King Solomon wrote, "Stay away from a fool, for you will not find the knowledge on their lips."[31] Does this statement make sense? I think it does. We have so many people who keep company and associations with fools. As a result, they only consume ignorance. They never mind acquiring knowledge. Jim Rohn says, "Learning is the beginning of wealth. Learning is the beginning of health. Learning is the beginning of spirituality. Searching and learning are where the miracle process all begins." I believe that health matters seem a simple issue for many people, but I think it is a serious issue needing careful attention. People never care about their health, but I will remind you that your health is vital. You can lose money or many things in life, but if your health fails, then you have lost everything. You will have lost the dreams, plans and vision. Here are some reasons why health matters:

---

31   Proverbs 14:7.

Health affects your emotional, intellectual and spiritual well-being.

Psychologists and behavioral scientists have reported that a human being has three components: body, soul and spirit. The physical body is like a container; it keeps soul and spirit. If the physical body is not healthy, then it is likely to suffer from disease or other ailments. Your physical body must be taken care of by doing physical exercises and maintaining a healthy lifestyle. The soul comprises of the emotions, mind and heart. To take care of your feelings and thoughts, you need to regularly and consistently understand your feelings as well as exercise your brain through acquiring correct information. Negative emotions also affect health, which requires you to manage your feelings. People who fail to control emotions are often negative and easily irritated. They never appreciate anything; the look for faults and blame others consistently. In the end, their relations break and become unrepairable.

Health determines your productivity in life.

Have you ever imagined a situation in which you or a family member is bedridden or hospitalized for several months or years? I read a story of a lady who was bedridden for 16 years. This lady had children but was utterly unable to help herself. For all those years, she was wholly unproductive and became a liability to her family and nation. The government had to spend money to keep her alive. Such things as poor health does happen to us with or without our knowledge or cause. Poor health can be due to several factors, including our lifestyles and responsibilities. The lesson here is that your health determines your capacity to produce or contribute to the human or national progress. Without good health, it is impossible to be productive in any area of life, including raising a family or making an impact or contribution to the betterment of life.

Health influences your capacity to exploit your potential in life.

Every human being has potential. The concept of possibility is one of the most significant discoveries that I know. Potential is what you have not done yet compared to what you have done. For instance, if you have a bachelor's degree, it means you have the potential for a master's and doctorate. If you have talents, gifts and ideas that you have not utilized, those are the potentials trying to manifest. If you have poor health, then you will not be able to release and exploit your potential. People who have good health can maximize their potential and achieve their purpose in life.

Health determines if your purpose and vision are reached.

God creates people for a reason. Your goal is what you are designed and produced to do. People with good health has potential to fulfill their mission and achieve their vision. On the other hand, people without good health have limitations to the achievement of their dreams. My purpose is to equip and empower aspiring leaders to serve humanity. My goal determines my lifestyle. Everything I do about my health is related to my mission and vision. My health influences my choices, habits and behavior. I made some decision years ago never to smoke, drink or engage in harmful behaviors because all those things can sabotage my plans and affect my destiny or future. I also discovered that my future is not ahead of me; it is trapped or hidden in me. I am like a seed whose future is buried on the inside. If I destroy my health, it means I am ruining my future.

Health determines the quality and quantity of life.

Do you know people or friends who spent every evening or weekend drinking? What can you say about their health? What about people who smoked every day for 10 or 20 years? What observations do you have about them? The worst thing about drinking or smoking and other vices is doing it excessively. You have people say, "Too much of everything is dangerous." Too much smoking and drinking are dangerous. Some of the early causes of death are excessive smoking or drinking. Others become older in appearance than those similarly aged before their time due to poor health management associated with health problems.

Good health is more natural to maintain than recover from lousy health.

Good health is a byproduct of lifestyle. As noted above, a lot of people spend their lives seeking and searching for earthly things: wealth, pleasure and happiness through various activities. Sometimes, people reach their goals at the cost of their health. I know people who spend hours working without time for recovery or rest. Permanent health problems include chronic diseases. It is normal to fall sick, but some illnesses can cause permanent health problems that become irreversible. It is that reason I believe that good health is more natural to keep then recovering from ill health.

Making The Lifelong Decision To Have Good Health

I vividly recall the day in the year 2010 when I visited the United Nations clinic in Kololo Hill, a suburb of Uganda's capital city, Kampala. A doctor carried out medical tests on me. At that time, I had not been feeling so well, and it had lasted about two months. I decided that I must see a physician at the UN clinic. The results revealed that I was having high blood pressure and diabetic levels. This surprised me. It became a wake-up call for me to act. From that time, I decided to adjust my lifestyle, and today, I feel my health is better than it was during those years. I decided to do the following:

- Listen to inspirational messages to keep a positive attitude.
- Read inspirational books to program my mindset.

- Eat the correct quantity and quality of meals every day.
- Get rest and enough sleep. Good sleep is good for life.
- Do periodic medical checkup at least every year.

Health Life Style

A healthy life is a personal choice and decision. Nobody knows how long he or she shall be alive, but living a long life and having good health all boil down to having a clear plan. In 2016, I was leaving with my family in Nairobi. There was an old lady, 68 years old. From first glance, you might think she is 25 years old, but her secret was doing regular exercises, eating fruits and maintaining a healthy diet. I learned from her that she does not eat what everyone eats. She is selective. In Kenya, the primary food is nyamachoma and ugali (posho and beef). Although they are typical and enjoyable, the problem associated with them is that they give a lot of kilocalories that are associated with weight gain and other diseases.

The greatest secret is that you must be selective about what you eat if you are going to keep away from diseases. Mark Twain says, "The only way to keep healthy is to eat what you do not want, drink what you don't like, and to do what you'd rather not." I agree with this message. Most people like to eat beef, drink beer or soft drinks, eat chocolate and avoid physical exercises. Those who do the opposite have a better lifestyle. The best advice I have for you is to moderate what you eat.

Things You Can Do to Improve Your Health

1. **Manage stress effectively:** Learn the factors that cause stress for you or family and find ways of managing those factors. Learn to manage problems, deal with difficulties, handle disappointments and manage people in your life.

2. **Daily physical activity or exercise:** Health workers recommend that regular physical activity increase opportunities for better health. Always practice this and results will be surprising. For my case, every day I make sure I do a simple activity to make me sweat. You can do a 30-60 minutes of physically activity. The results will be amazing.

3. **Eat rightly:** Watch your meals and avoid food that cause you problems.

4. **Laugh and relax:** Always find time for social activities where you relax; create a work-life balance.

The Choice to Live a Life of Health

I believe that everyone is born with capacities to make choices and decisions. If someone has a desire to change their lives, they can. For instance, everyone can dream dreams, succeed, achieve or be fruitful. The most significant problems are the lack of knowledge or ignorance and negligence. Some people accept the status quo; they allow circumstances to control them. For instance, they blame their parents, background, personal mistakes, errors in judgment or poor decision-making capacities. Maybe you disagree with me about these things.

In this chapter, I am writing about health. Health information is available, but some people do not know about it; they are ignorant or negligent. They never search for information or knowledge. There is an ancient adage that those who seek will find, those who know the door opens and those who search will get. Hence, education of health and other areas is available. If people take personal responsibility for their situation, then life begins to change. Without personal change, there can be no change. If you desire to be and do better in life, then you must become better first. If you want an extraordinary experience, then you must do extraordinary things. There is a concept of value that I learned in an economics class in high school. I wrote about it in my book, *Becoming an Influential Leader: How to Gain and Sustain It with Others in Your generation.* In that book, I explained the concept of value as being the same as worth. Anything of value must be paid. People spend millions, dollars, pounds or any currency on oil, gold, diamonds and others because of their costs. A person of value is more attractive than the one without.

Someone asked me a question: How does one change? My answer was to change; it does not have to start with a big step. All that is needed is to start with small steps in the right direction with self-discipline based on values. There are many ways to change your life. That choice is yours.

Total Well-Being

You cannot have a healthy life without having complete or total well-being. The overall well-being involves the health of the three parts or layers. Psychologists and behavioral scientists have argued that a human being or a person has three parts:

1. **Body:** Physical structure or container.
2. **Soul:** Intellect, emotions and will.
3. **Spirit:** Eternal and transcends the world.

A healthy life must have a complete balance in all the three parts. The three areas are interdependent. Some people take care of the physical body and neglect the other two or another way around. Some people work only on the intellect or emotions. One of my mentors told me a statement that I will never forget about feelings. He was sharing about the story of Moses's failure to reach the Promised Land when instead of controlling his emotions, he allowed emotions to control him. My mentor said understanding controls emotions. Emotions come from feelings. Human feelings come from the senses: taste, sight, touch, smell, and sound. Human perception and response to what happens around their surrounding come from any or combination of those five senses. If you can understand your emotions, then you can control them. Most people who act irrationally allow emotions to take over. As a result, they have landed in problems or canceled their destinies in life.

Meanwhile, intellect is kept healthy through acquiring the right information and knowledge. If a person does not get the correct information, then there is the danger of ignorance. The cause of many problems in life is ignorance. Some solutions to problems are resolved by acquiring knowledge without even going to see a doctor, psychologist or a counselor. The will is the decision maker. The power of choice and will are the most dangerous gifts that God ever gave humankind. An intention to decide is a dominant force. Humankind can choose to love or not love God or fellow man. Humankind has that power and it is impossible to take it away. These three parts can be considered as an onion. The onion has different layers. The outer one is the physical body. The middle one is the soul. The inner one is the spirit. The spiritual health is sustained through having beliefs, faith, prayers, singing worship songs, reading holy books and association with religious organizations or churches and mosques among others. Physical health is sustained by merely doing regular physical activities such as running, swimming, walking, jogging and any exercises that allow the body to sweat. Once you sweat, there is a feeling that emerges after all these complicated things. Often seen from the outside only, good health reflects what is on the inside.

Finally, to have a healthy life, there must be a significant focus on working on the three parts: body, soul and spirit. As each of them gets exercised, they become secure and robust. Mahatma Gandhi said, "It is health that is the real wealth and not pieces of gold and silver."[32]

---

32   https://www.goodreads.com/quotes/7067021-it-is-health-that-is-real-wealth-and-not-pieces

Chapter 11

IDEAS

Great minds discuss ideas; average minds discuss events;
small minds discuss people.
– Eleanor Roosevelt

Do You Read Books?

How many have you read last month or even last year? I am always reading books related to my areas of interest for the past 15 years. The two areas of my interest are leadership and management. The main reasons for my desire to read books are to acquire ideas, expand my opportunities, increase my influence and grow as a leader. The most significant sources of ideas are books. There are millions of books that have been written from the time of the first civilization until this day. The books are containers of knowledge, ideas, and information. Books have ideas about anything that can change your life, situation and circumstances. They contain facts, principles, rules, stories and precepts. Books contain concepts that come from thoughts. Everything that I know in life, I either learned from books or from people. However, many people around the world are not achieving their dreams, potential and visions because they are ignorant. Some of them do not know. If you have ideas, then you are on your way to the top of life. Remember this wise saying: "The bottom is always overcrowded, so always try to get on top of life."

In addition, it has been said that leaders are readers and readers are leaders. If you want to lead in area, you must read books related to that area. Have you ever imagined how many books have been published in history? Let me share with you what I found from my research. Google has estimated that as of 2010, approximately 130,000,000 distinct titles have been published[33]. There could be more books written but not published. Can you imagine? The global population is currently about 7.5 billion; only a small proportion of the people have gotten opportunities to read or attend school.

Suppose you want to be an accountant; then read accounting books. Suppose you want to be the best cook; then read books about cooking. Suppose you want to be the best parent; then read books about parenting. Suppose you want to be the best teacher; then read books about teaching. Suppose you want to be a community worker; then read books related to community or social work. Suppose you want to be a lawyer; then read books related to law. Suppose you want to become an engineer; then read books related to engineering. If you're going to be a security officer, read security or crime books. If you want to be a politician or economist, then you need books on politics and economics. Suppose you want to be a manager or administrator; then read books on management and administration. Whatever area you are interested in; you can read books on those topics.

One of the most fabulous ideas I ever heard was, "The poorest person on Earth is one without a dream. Moreover, the most frustrated person is

---

33   https://mashable.com/2010/08/05/number-of-books-in-the-world/#x54rwcIFPmqH

the one whose vision has not been fulfilled." If a person is poor, then the problem is the lack of ideas. Every person has a factory called the brain or mind that is designed to produce ideas. When those ideas are created, they can transform the whole world. Let me get practical about the concept of ideas. First, ideas come from thoughts. When you engage in thinking, the results of your thinking process will be many thoughts and ideas. Thinking and reflection are essential. Thinking gives your ideas or opinions. Those ideas or thoughts can change your life. If they are good or great thoughts, guess what happens: a good life. If they are bad thoughts, then imagine what you will receive: a lousy life. Good thoughts or ideas enable you to make right decisions. Right decisions always lead to a useful life. Every person is the sum or total of all the decisions and choices they have made. From this, I can conclude that thinking is a critical requirement for a successful life.

Every person is the sum or total of all the decisions and choices they have made over the time they have lived.

I believe the most powerful thing on Earth is ideas. Ideas are the source of everything. Ideas create problems and solutions. For instance, the problem of transport was solved by an idea that Henry Ford and the Wright brothers had when they created automobiles and airplanes respectively. The problem of communication was solved when Alexander Graham Bell invented the first telephone. The problem of lighting was solved when Thomas Edison worked hard to make a light bulb. All over the world, people use bulbs in homes, offices, airplanes, cars and streets among others. If you look around your house, office or community, you will realize that ideas produced everything that you have around you (for instance, the bed, chairs, desks, clothes, shoes, watches, eyeglasses, earphones, cameras, smartphones, smartwatches, books, pens, glasses, computers, fringes, refrigerators, cars, and so forth). Everything that humans use today started with an idea that someone decided to pursue. Great companies or businesses were ideas. Great buildings or projects were born out ideas and so on. I mean everything.

Thinking is one of the pillars that you need in life. Let me put it differently: You need to think so you can have ideas. In this case, ideas are also a pillar of life.

Changes in the World

As you might have noticed, the world is changing every day, and those changes are going to be unprecedented or uncontrollable. Nobody has the power to stop the change, and those changes are going to affect every corner of the world. The most affected person might be you. However, what is driving the change? Change in the world is driven by ideas. A person with a great idea will affect the world. A person who can see the problems as opportunities can apply their ideas to solve the problems. A person without an idea cannot affect anything in the world. For instance, Steve Jobs' idea of a smartphone completely changed the world. For innovation and expansion to be attained, there must be new ideas. Any new change will be created when new ideas are pursued and translated to become a reality. A good thinker will develop ideas that can affect and impact the world. They translate their thoughts into ideas and then produce whatever they want. Good and better ideas create a good or better world. However, the opposite is also true. Bad ideas also create a bad world. For instance, poverty, terrorism, criminal minds and the like cause problems.

*A good thinker will create ideas
that can affect and impact the world.*

The nature of ideas:

- Ideas emerge out of thinking.
- Ideas submerge and remerge.
- Ideas cannot be killed.
- Ideas can affect the world.
- Ideas never die if documented or brought to life.

Let me state something that is aimed at tickling your mind. Every day, things are changing and a new set of circumstances are changing. All of these require thinking. Thinking must never be an end, but rather a process. It is an ongoing process. You must continuously think to find solutions to problems, manage circumstances, manage change and manage people around you. Shoddy thinking is the cause of man's failure to solve problems. Every problem has a solution. That solution, however, will require ideas. Then, you must select the best idea from the many ideas to solve the problem. If you have a problem, then it means you have a problem thinking. You are not generating ideas and selecting the best ones to apply.

Furthermore, successful people in life are those who manage and do their thinking. Succeeding in life requires that you must do your thinking effectively. There is no magic about thinking. It is a doorway to unlimited ideas and solutions to every problem. One major reason why problems persist is because of poor or little thinking. Moreover, throughout all generations, ideas are always emerging and submerging. Those who have ideas succeed. There is no formula for success. The principles are the same throughout all generations. King Solomon wrote, "What has been will be again, what has been done will be done again; there is nothing new under the sun."[34] Everything that exists is a product of innovation and creativity of some individuals. Those individuals have the same brain capacity and number of cells as everyone else. For instance, Steve Jobs, Bill Gates, Thomas Edison and others who have contributed to great innovations all have the same minds as all humans, but they simply think differently.

Why Some People Never Pursue Their Ideas

I think it is important to comment on this. So many ideas are never pursued and are buried in the cemetery. There are many reasons for that. One of those reasons is fear. Another reason is fear of rejection or success. People come up with all sorts of questions. What if it does not work? What will people say? Some people discard their ideas because of comments from others who say their ideas will never work out. As a result, they give up. However, here is the truth: Your ideas are possible. You can achieve your dreams. You can fight to achieve the ideas or dreams that you have been having. There are some things you need to know. You must prepare for hard times, setbacks, challenges, attacks or problems as you pursue your ideas. There are countless examples of people who had ideas but gave up.

---

34   Ecclesiastes 1:9.

However, there are also few people who never gave up their ideas or dreams. One of them is Thomas Edison, he failed 1,000 times and then the 1,001st attempt is when he succeeded to make a light bulb. Another great leader in history, Jesus Christ, had an idea of saving humanity. He paid the price of the cross and said, "It is finished." Some people have accepted the opinion of others as reality, and they have given up on their ideas. Let me tell you: Your ideas are possible. You can achieve your dreams or ideas. Your ideas can produce things or change the world. You should never accept the limitations of your mind or circumstances to dictate or stop you from running after your ideas. As we have seen, ideas change the world. Everything comes from ideas. Ideas are your desires. They keep burning you until you achieve them you cannot be satisfied or fulfilled. Fight for your ideas; never be satisfied and never give up on your idea. Some people give up because they think the idea is wrong. No, it's not. Your ideas are possible.

Why Do Ideas Matter Every Day?

Before I share my thoughts about the significance of ideas or add on some additional points, let me suggest this: Learn to think on paper or books; do not trust your mind. Ideas or thoughts are like birds that can fly next to you but quickly fly away. If you are not prepared to catch the birds, they will fly away and leave you alone. Most people think or trust their brains too much. In fact, some of the ideas that I share or present in my books come from when I am walking or doing physical exercises. However, when I do those things and inspiration strikes, I dash to write the ideas in my books and then continue to think and expand. This formula has worked for me. It has also worked for many people that have changed the world.

Claude M. Bristol, the author of The Magic of Believing, said, "Thought is the original source of all wealth, all success, all material gain, all great discoveries and inventions, and achievements."[35] Is this not true? Do you disagree? For me, I agree. Nothing has ever been created or discovered without thoughts or ideas. Even the creation of the world in the Bible started with a word. A word is a hidden idea or thoughts. When a thought is spoken out, it becomes a word.

That's why the Bible says,

> *In the beginning was the Word, and the Word was with God, and the Word was God. He was with God in the beginning. Through Him all things were made; without Him, nothing was made that has been made. In him was life, and that life was the light of all humankind. The light shines in the darkness, and the darkness has not overcome it.*[36]

Now if you recall the concept of the Word being a hidden thought, then you rephrase that Scripture by it. God had a hidden thought or hidden idea. The hidden thought or idea created everything or all things. That is why it is difficult to finish people with an idea or thought. You can fight them, but if they pursue their thoughts or ideas, they will be different.

Have you made getting ideas a priority in life? Have you made thinking a part of your daily existence? If not, then you are missing on something very critical. I am suggesting that you start today buying books, so you get ideas instead of filling your mind with things that are not necessary. To improve your life, you need to start by deciding to get ideas or think every day. Then you make another decision to discipline yourself and practice that habit daily. Let's look at some reasons or benefits for getting ideas.

---

35   Claude M. Bristol, *The Magic of Believing* (New York: Pocket Books, 1994).
36   John 5:1-5.

Good ideas produce good results

You cannot have anything of lasting value without having a good idea. Everything good comes from good ideas. For every idea, it comes from thinking that was done. No achievement or accomplishment happens, but it always precedes thinking. Success never comes by accident. People never fall into success or achievements; they first engage in the thinking before they realize it. The level of success increases if you place high value and price on thinking. The greater your capacity to generate ideas, the greater your chances of success. The greater your thinking, the greater your potential for growth. Victor Hugo said, "A small man is made up of small thoughts."37 This is possibly the reason why most people are too small.

Good ideas increase your value

Any person who possesses good ideas has the capacity to provide solutions to problems. Even in large or small organizations, those with ideas are always rewarded while those without ideas are easily let go. Organizations have employees with knowledge, skills, talents and experience. However, those with new ideas have more value. The good news is that anybody can get ideas. The most important thing is that you have ideas and those ideas can help you navigate through life or business. All great companies or countries have been born or founded on ideas. Ideas are the foundation of great businesses or nations. Everything built or resulting in advancement is founded on ideas. A person who is a good thinker always has good ideas. A good thinker is a more valuable person than a bad thinker.

Poor ideas make people slaves

People who not free are slaves. Also, people who are not developing or growing are those who never take time to think. They often find themselves at the painful mercy of their surroundings or circumstances. They are incapable of handling, dealing or solving problems. They also meet

---

37   https://vision.org.au/the-word-for-today/2017/09/16/become-a-good-thinker/

obstacles that stop them because they cannot determine the way out. An old German proverb says, "Better an empty purse than an empty head."[38] If you are a good thinker, you will always overcome difficulties and setbacks even if you have no resources or funds. However, if you are a poor thinker, you will lack confidence. You can be easily intimidated and may find yourself at the mercy of the great thinkers. One of my secrets when I am faced with difficulties is to get a book and read. When I read, I will find ideas that will inspire or motivate me. In other words, good ideas give me a positive attitude.

Make A Decision To Get Ideas

Every day or when I am traveling or flying, I am always carrying physical books or e-books. I started to value education when I had completed my primary education. My late mother always told me, "Education is the key to success." I recall when I had gone with her to my uncle, the late Mzee Samuel Willian Odeke, she was requesting for a cow to be sold for me to get tuition to join high school. After the meeting, we walked back to her parents' home. On the way, she said, "Son, education will open doors for you." I never forgot those words. One of the books that gave me life and hope was a Good News Bible. It had ideas and principles that have guided my life over all the years. What books are you reading? If you desire to obtain ideas, then your daily life should be guided by following:

Understand that ideas come from thinking

If you cannot spend the time to think, you will less likely get ideas. Most people spend time watching bad news or listening to music or doing activities that never help them get ideas. As such, they continue with old ideas. Old ideas are like old clothes; they never make you smart. New ideas are like new clothes; you see yourself as intelligent and attractive. To get good ideas, you must become a good thinker, and to get great ideas, you

---

38   https://vision.org.au/the-word-for-today/2017/09/16/become-a-good-thinker/

must become a great thinker. Through practice and persistent reading and learning, you can become a great thinker who produces excellent ideas. As you think, ideas will start flowing. If you get smarter, then you will have great ideas.

Manage your weaknesses and maximize your strength.

Every person has weaknesses and strengths. Assess your strengths and weaknesses. You need to develop an appetite for reading. It is possible. You have millions of brain cells. You have good eyes. You can write the key points that you read. You can start a journal. You can master what you read. You can reflect on what you learn, and when you get the ideas, write them down. Continue in this manner until you become a master or champion.

Types Of Thinking You Must Learn

Let me start by explaining the concept of thinking. Thinking refers to the cognitive activities you use to process information, solve problems, make decisions and create new ideas. You use your thinking skills when you try to make sense of experiences, organize, ask questions, make plans or decide what to do. The following are the various forms of thinking:

1. **Creative Thinking:** This refers to the ability to conceive new and innovative ideas by breaking from established thoughts, theories, rules and procedures. It involves putting together, in new and imaginative ways. Creative thinking is often referred to as "thinking outside the box."

2. **Analytical Thinking:** This refers to the ability to separate a whole into its basic parts to examine the parts and their relationships. It involves thinking in a logical, step-by-step manner to break down a large system of information into parts.

3. **Critical Thinking:** This refers to the ability to exercise careful evaluation or judgment to determine the authenticity, accuracy, worth, validity, reliability or value of something. In addition to precise, objective analysis, critical thinking involves synthesis, evaluation, reflection and reconstruction. Moreover, rather than strictly breaking down the information, critical thinking explores other elements that could have an influence on the conclusion.

4. **Concrete Thinking:** This refers to the ability to comprehend and apply factual knowledge. It is about thinking of objects or ideas as specific items rather than as a theoretical representation of a more general concept. It involves everything on the surface—always literal or plain and to the point.

5. **Abstract Thinking:** This refers to the ability to use concepts to make and understand generalization then relating or connecting them to other items, events or experiences. It involves paying attention to hidden meanings, thus allowing you to observe and understand theories and possibilities.

6. **Divergent Thinking:** This is the ability to generate creative ideas by exploring many solutions possible to find facts and data together from various sources and then applying logic and knowledge to solve problems or make decisions. It starts from a common point and moves outwards in divergent or different directions to involve a variety of aspects or perspectives.

7. **Convergent Thinking:** This refers to the ability to put together several different pieces or perspectives of a topic together in some organized, logical manner to find a single answer. It involves focusing on a future number of solutions rather than proposing multiple solutions.

8. **Sequential (Linear) Thinking:** This is the ability to process information in an orderly, prescribed manner. It involves a step-by-step progression where the response to a step must be obtained before another step is taken.

9. **Holistic (Non-Linear) Thinking:** This is the ability to see the big picture and recognize the interconnectedness of various components that form the larger system. It involves expanding your thoughts process in multiple directions rather than in just one direction and understanding a system by sensing its patterns. Tools such as SWOT, PESTEL and SOAR are used for holistic thinking. Holistic thinking is also referred to as "Big picture thinking."

10. **Strategic Thinking:** This is the ability to develop long-term goals for three, five or 10 years and plans their achievement to increase opportunities, solve problems and manage changes in the environments.

11. **Reflective Thinking:** This is the ability to review and revisit the past ideas, look at the past perspectives, gain more understanding of relationships and take decisions.

12. **Possibility Thinking:** The ability to think through passion, enthusiasm and finding solutions to problems that seem impossible or difficult situations. "What if" is asked repeatedly until solutions are found.

13. **Focused Thinking:** This is the ability to think on issues and remove distractions clearly as well as all mental clutters or garbage from the mindset. It requires concentration, discipline and focus.

14. **Design Thinking:** This refers to the technique used by people (especially engineers) to design technically or produce prototypes from their imagination, thoughts or ideas.

From the various approaches to thinking, it is advisable not to rely on a single type. That will narrow down and limit the human potential to solve problems, make decisions or objectively progress. The use of one approach limits a person as they might disregard outcomes of other types of thinking options. Academicians and other scholars often have a rigid approach to thinking. I am sorry to be writing this here.

How to Manage the Discipline to Get Ideas

I have learned that it is straightforward for people to influence others. It is also easy to allow setbacks, problems and circumstances to affect your ability to think or create ideas. That is what is killing many people. They are overwhelmed by problems. Most people allow others to influence them. They seek ideas and perspectives over issues from others. This is dangerous because people always have hidden motives and agendas different from yours. The wise thing to do is to rely on yourself and trusted friends. You must take personal responsibility to seek ideas or knowledge. When I was a teenager, I started to master the concept of getting my ideas. I never had many people who ever advised me on what to do. Even in high school, I always made my own decisions, based on what I had learned and read. For you to generate ideas, you must do the following:

1. **Identity a place where you can think.** It is essential to get a place where you can think or reflect. You cannot be in a noisy environment and expect to get good ideas. You need to be in a serene setting. Most of the great men in history got solutions when they were in an isolated environment. Archimedes discovered what became "Eureka! The Archimedes Principle" while he was lying in

a bathtub. He got a solution to a problem that had failed for several weeks. It is also reported that Isaac Newton discovered the laws of motion when he was by himself. The same applied to the law of gravity when Galileo was seated under a mango tree. For instance, I am alone in Abbey 5 in Chelsea Village in Mogadishu as I write this book. My family is far away in Uganda, and I am using every opportunity to think and work on my ideas. You must create a plan that works for you and apply it. No one is going to create a system for your life. You are responsible for designing your destiny.

2. **Allocate time for thinking each day.** You cannot get your good ideas all the time. You must learn when you can think effectively. For instance, for me, some ideas I get while running on a treadmill, jogging or early morning after I have slept and rested. I do this often and I keep a record of my thoughts. I never trust my mind.

3. **Create your personal system.** All people are not the same. The way I approach life or do things may not be the same as you. You have the power to decide how you plan to get ideas. You are master and driver of your life. You determine your destiny. In all, you must decide what approach is best for you.

4. **Capture your ideas or thoughts.** It is important that you write down your ideas or thoughts so that you avoid losing them. Ideas come as birds that visit your balcony or compound but quickly fly away. If I get a good idea, I transfer it to my journal. If I am sleeping at night and I get an idea, I will rush to the living room to take of it and return to continue with my sleep.

5. **Think positively all the time, avoid negative thoughts.** Anyone can be good at thinking, but unless you focus on positive thoughts,

it will be a waste of efforts. If you are constantly thinking, worrying and wailing about everything, then you are likely to produce negative thoughts. As we have seen, negative thoughts never lead you anywhere good. They cannot produce success but instead can cause you a failure. You can always start to think about the dreams or plans you want to achieve.

6. **Learn that garbage in is garbage out.** Whatever you put in to your mind is what you get out. There is ancient wisdom that whatever you sow, you will reap. This is a universal principle in life. If you think of good ideas, you will have them. I personally do much reading. When I am stressed or faced with enormous challenges, my medicine is either read or sleep. However, when I wake up, I will have right ideas.

7. **Associate with people who think big; then you can think big and achieve big things.** You have heard that birds of the same feathers flock together? This is true. If you spend time with wise people, you will end up being wise too. I am always conscious of the people I spend time with. Another way is to read books of great people and top thinkers. In this way, you begin to think like them. The exposure to their ideas and wisdom will also influence your thoughts.

What My Thinking Has Done To Me

I applied the concept of reflective thinking about which I have written. The benefits for me include:

- My thinking enabled me to focus on my future positively with hope.
- My thinking helped me to disengage or separate from my negative peers.
- My thinking produced ideas, beliefs, and convictions.

- My thinking helped me understand various concepts, principles, and terms.
- My thinking helped me know my gifts, capacities, potential, and purpose.
- My thinking helped me at work and university as well as handle life's difficulties.
- My thinking has taken me to a higher level, including becoming a writer and author.

Final Advice

It does not matter where you originate. Your circumstances or situation is not different from others. I believe you have the capacity to get ideas. Follow these concepts and change your thinking. A change in your thinking will change your life. Your life is controlled by the way you think. Apostle Paul wrote to the Romans believers, "Do not conform to the pattern of this world but be transformed by the renewing of your mind. Then you will be able to test and approve what God's will is—his good, pleasing and perfect will."[39] The message that I get from Apostle Paul is that transformation comes from the renewing of your mind.

If you renew your mind, so much will happen. You could be in stressful situations or circumstances. However, I can assure you there is still a future and a hope. You might not have achieved your goals or encountered setbacks. If you can change your thinking, you generate ideas that give you an advantage. That is where your life can turn around and become a better one because you have unlimited potential hidden in you.

---

39   Romans 12:2

Chapter 12

MONEY

Money is not the only answer, but it makes a difference
— ***Barack Obama,***

Former President of the United States.

What Do You Know About Money Or Finance?

Everyone on Earth always has a desire to have money in his or her lives. Some people worship money while others do not. Some people want it badly, others only fairly. I have never met a person who does not want money. I know a few people who have too much and can give it away easily. Every person wants money; they do whatever it takes to acquire money. Money or finance is critical because it facilitates exchange or trade. The concept of money is as old as the time of creation. The Bible has Scriptures about money such as Genesis 17:12-13, 23, Genesis 42:35, Genesis 47:14-18 and Exodus 21:11 among others. As a young Christian in Mbale High School, the Scripture that really caught my attention was Apostle Paul's message of caution to Timothy: "For the love of money is a root of all kinds of evil. Some people, eager for money, have wandered from the faith and pierced themselves with many griefs."[40] Paul said loving money is a root cause of all kinds of evil and this is true for people without strong values and principles. Our focus must never be to love money but only to love God. If you study the lives of people who love money, they never care about others or people. A lot of people have put their faith in money instead of God; when the money goes away they commit suicide.

Life Without Much Money

In High School I used to live in Namatala, a slum in Mbale that was closer to the Mbale High Schools where I was studying. I also lived in our rural villages of Miroi and Akuoro in Bukedea district, where my mother and father were born respectively. As you might have read in my story, we were poor and everyone else was poor according to what I saw as a little boy. We had cattle, goats and sheep as a source of wealth. As a young boy, I thought we were wealthy. In the late 1980s, however, the impact of cattle raids by the Karamojong, a neighboring tribe in Eastern Uganda, left many families poor, including ours.

When I was in high school, I was privileged to study economics. In economics class, we studied theories on the wealth of nations and how wealth is measured. I recall one day, we had a mental exercise to estimate our wealth, then I realized everyone was poor. That analysis really stuck with me, and even though having cattle is a source of pride among people in my tribe, Iteso, I had an understanding that we lived with poverty. Imagine having so many cows whose value cannot even give you much wealth. If you are from Eastern Uganda, you can do a simple mathematics analysis to determine the value of cows at the current market prices in your local

---

40   1 Timothy 6:10.

market. A big bull in my community, for example, costs about $400; most people have not more than 500 cows. That means a family can have $20,000 as their wealth. Is this a lot?

What Does Money Really Do?

Having come far in life of which I am unashamed, I have had opportunities to have money and travel to many countries. I have been to the USA, Spain, Netherlands and Belgium. I used to imagine or think that everyone in those countries is rich or wealthy, but the reality is that even rich or wealthy nations have poor people or beggars. As much as they have wealthy people, they also have people who struggle in life without necessities. Based on that introduction, let me share what money does and what it does not do. Here are a few lessons to think about.

Money solves problems but does not solve all problems of life on Earth. All people have problems, including the wealthy or rich people in your neighborhood. One of the owners of the biggest shopping malls in Nairobi in Kenya is wealthy, or the richest man in the country. When I was in Kenya, I was informed that he was diagnosed with cancer and was dying soon. I thought about this guy for a whole afternoon and concluded that he has a health problem but not money problems. His money cannot solve all his problems. What must be noted is that even though the rich people have what poor people think of as everything, they also have problems and not everything. There are some things that they also long to have or wish to have, but they cannot have it all. Even though rich people might have millions in their bank accounts, own properties, airplanes, hotels, investments, drive the latest cars and travel in first class, they still have problems.

◇◇◇

Even though rich people might have millions in their bank accounts, own properties, airplanes, hotels, investments, drive the latest cars and travel in first class, they still have problems.

◇◇◇

Some people that I have met, want to have money badly. They want to be millionaires or billionaires, but they are not willing to work hard and sacrifice. They keep wishing they could become millionaires and billionaires. Too many people think, including me, that money provides you with choices or options. It gives you a chance to make a difference. It gives you opportunities. It gives you security and stability. Some families have broken down because the men are without money: "He was unable to meet the family needs." Here is what also happens to money:

- Money can always go away in time; there is nothing permanent.
- Money can be lost; you can lose it anytime.
- Money can be stolen or abused.
- Money can be "eaten" by inflation.
- Money can lose value.
- Money can be borrowed or saved.
- Even wealthy or rich people can become bankrupt, including millionaires and billionaires.

What Should You Do with Money?

Here are some ideas; you might disagree, which is your choice:

- Give money to people; you will influence and eventually lead them.
- Never money become your everything; because when you lose it, you have lost everything.
- Learn how to make more money as you become a millionaire or billionaire, so when you lose it, then you can still become either of the two. You can give a million away and still have the capacity to make a million.
- Never stress about money, but work on the idea. Money follows people who work on ideas. Money does not go to people who are stressed. Financial pressure can take a toll on people, hence affecting their work ethics, productivity and concentration.

How to Make Money

The next thing I want to write about is how to make money. There is an adage; "Whoever loves money, never has enough money."[41] There are many ways people make money; others make money through working for it or stealing it. If you steal money, it means you lack values; there are chances that you will have regrets in your future. If you are working genuinely, it means you have strong values and you are likely not to regret your actions. The greatest secret to making money is something that most business schools never teach their students. If you want to make money, the get an idea and pursue it. The idea could be to solve a problem. If you solve a problem or satisfy a need, you are likely to become a tycoon. Those who work for others often receive salaries and wages, but those who work on their own earn profits. They have invested their time to create their own brand or company; now they enjoy the sweat of their labor. The two systems for making money are salary and the profit system.

---

41   Ecclesiastes 5:10.

How To Start Making Money

Like everything in life, it does not need to be big; you can look at how you started life. I remember how a friend of mine started a cake business. It started in our house. It started small, but believe me, it started with passion, devotion, sacrifice, commitment, learning, consistency and persistence; the business started growing and expanding. The opportunities started to emerge, from giving cakes or cookies for free to receiving orders from customers. Today, that business is expanding; opportunities and challenges are also being experienced.

Here is the principle: If you work on your idea with determination, you will make money. You will either have a product or service that people will pay for and you will earn money. You must also remember that anything of value is always costly. Scarce things or products are costly or valuable, but common goods, products and services are cheap. If you decide to work on your ideas, you will experience discomfort or pain, but that pain is better than regrets of not working on your ideas. There are two types of pain: the pain of discipline and the pain of regret. You choose which type you want.

Achieving Financial Freedom

Most people dream of being financially free, but they are never working towards it. Financial freedom or independence is when you can sustain your life with income that gained from personal resources and investments. If you do not have that capacity, then you are not financially free. Financial independence simply implies you pay yourself from your personal investments. Financial dependence means that someone takes the obligation to pay you.

Facts About Money

Things that I have learned about money are:

1. **Money will never be enough.** Nobody has enough money. Even the richest person or nation on Earth still needs money.

2. **Sometimes, money will not make you happy.** The reason has been said: Money can buy you a house, but not a home. Researchers have concluded that the more money one gets; the more problems they experience; it does not bring true happiness. Henry Ford said, "Money doesn't change men; it merely unmasks them. If a man is naturally selfish, or arrogant, or greedy, the money brings it out; that's all."

3. **Borrowed money can be a blessing or a curse.** If you pay it, then you are blessed, but if you fail, it affects your relationships, especially if you got it from friends.

4. **Money gives you choices or options.** If you are poor, then you have no idea or dream. Ideas or dreams are building blocks to getting money. A poor person has limited or few options.

5. **Making money should never be a goal.** The goal should be to use the money to impact lives.

How To Allocate Your Funds Or Income?

Experience is always the best teacher. Mistakes are the greatest teachers in life. Without mistakes, you will not learn much. I made mistakes personally when I started earning my income. As a result of a long search, I figured out the best formula which I now apply on personal income as below:

- Give to the church its 10 percent.
- Give charity about 10 percent.

- Give personal development and self-improvement 15 percent.
- Give investment 20 percent.
- Give living expenses 45 percent.

The Impact of Poverty

When I started to work in early 2000, I had a lot of learning to do, and I had just graduated from Makerere University. I had an opportunity to study a project planning course in which I was confronted with real facts about poverty and its situation in Uganda. During that class, the course facilitator or trainer said something that I have not forgotten about poverty. He said, "Poverty makes you hopeless, defenseless and powerless." In the same course, I also learned about the various types of poverty such as physical poverty, mental, social, spiritual and economic poverty. My initial thoughts about poverty were based on my childhood circumstances only relating to economic poverty, which is the absence of money or liquidity. This touched me, and I had to make decisions. One of those decisions was to sacrifice to save and invest my resources wisely without seeking instant success and gratification. I started to apportion my earning as per the above-mentioned formula. Nowadays, I see that my efforts are paying off. The best advice I can offer is that everyone who wants to become financially independent needs to learn how to earn and manage the resources they acquire, and with time, things will get better.

If you have difficulties doing this, then you can follow the following principles:

1. Attach value to things that you have such as assets and properties.
2. Identify where your money is going.
3. Check if you are making money.
4. Identify your worst or bad money habits or attitudes.
5. Work within your budget.

6. Avoid incurring debts.
7. Ensure consistent saving patterns, habits, and culture.
8. Learn to invest wisely. Your greatest investment must be in people, not things.
9. Remember money is seasonal; you will never have money all the time.
10. Learn more about money and how to earn; then explore ways to multiply the money. Do you remember the ancient story of a leader who gave talents to three people?

The Phases Of Life On Earth

I do not know how you have lived life up until this moment, but one thing I have learned is that life has seasons or phases as follows:

Step 1: Growing and Learning. The first phase is growing and learning. This phase is when your focus must be on getting knowledge and wisdom. In this phase, you study hard, identify your talent, discover your life's purpose and where you want to end in life. The primary goal of this phase is growing and learning. It is also personal development, self-improvement, character development, spiritual formation and development of your potential. No shortcuts at any phase is good because it negates or interferes with the future that is ahead of you as well as that which is trapped on the inside of you. Identify your life's values and principles. Learning to stand by those values and beliefs is critical. Other things to do could be crafting your life's plan and direction as well as choosing friends and dropping others.

Phase 2: Working and Earning. If you have acquired knowledge, wisdom, skills, and competencies, then you should be employed or pursuing your private mission or purpose. You also know your gift. Then you need to do it with excellence. The choice of your career has an impact on your earning ability and power. In phase 2 you also have a family not only to take care of, but also to plan their future. These happen generally when you are from age 25 forward.

Phase 3: Impacting and Returning. You never find happiness in your enjoyment alone. Joy comes when you have a big heart. If you have worked hard and planned well, then you can now start to impact and change the life of others. This phase is more rewarding. Being diligent and deliberate with patience allows you to move through these phases and your potential to maximize the other phases increased. Suppose you have not had a good foundation or start. Do not complain. Do not compete with anybody. Do not compare yourself with others.

Do the following things:
1. Focus on learning and growing.
2. Keep your discipline.
3. Keep your integrity.
4. Do not give up. If you give up, you will never go up, and you will only go down.

There is a tendency among people to rush from one phase to another. That must be avoided. This can be a source of problems because people never want to go through the process. We have so many young people who want instant success or gratification. You must know that every phase has its timing and the timing is decided and set by God. Take your time but keep moving. If you follow through carefully with commitment, then there are higher chances that you will finish well. If you neglect the advice, however, it is like a builder who rushes to build a house without a firm or solid foundation. When the wind or storms attack the house, it will collapse under pressure because the foundation is a week.

Debt Management

I had an experience of borrowing money from the bank and private money lenders. I not only borrowed money from two banks in Uganda at different times, but also from people who lend money. I had needs that I was unable to meet or cover. My experience with managing those debts made me realize my own mistakes. I learned that debts cause more problems than solutions. I realized that the debts make people helpless and hopeless. I also experienced sleepless nights when I had not completed repaying the money back.

If anyone is to get a loan or have debt, then it must be for acquiring things that appreciate such as purchasing land, property or houses at strategic locations. The debts can also be incurred if it is for purposes of saving time and increasing efficiency. For instance, you can buy a vehicle for convenience and to travel faster as well as buy computers for you to do your work more efficiently and effectively. You can also get loans or debts if you want to invest in education, personal development or starting a business. The bottom line, however, is to manage the debts very well.

Here are some of the lessons I learned about debts:

- Do not have loans to acquire things that never appreciate or increase in value.
- Pay your debts as required by following your repayment plan.
- Avoid getting debts or loans if at all possible unless you really must get it.
- Manage the cash that you have and know where your money is going.
- Develop a financial game plan.
- Take your time to invest the little resources you have, and they will grow.

- Seek financial advice. You do not know everything. If you are sick, you do not treat yourself; you get to the hospital or clinic to see a professional.

Financial Planning

There is an old saying that is so true: "Failing to plan is planning to fail." It is essential to develop a plan to manage your finances. Apply the financial formula that I have provided in this chapter. Also, develop the habit and discipline of investing as opposed to consumption. One of the reasons why poor people remain the way they are is the mindset. The poor think of consumption before investment. Someone once said that the only difference between the poor and the rich is that the rich invest their money and spend what is left, but the poor spend their money and invest what is left. Isn't this amazing?

To be honest, I am writing my experiences about financial planning even though I am not indeed an authority. I studied a postgraduate course at Uganda Management Institute. One of the modules was financial management and accounting. It was a great experience. I passed the class with an A+, but I think everything requires practice and continuous learning. If you do not practice something, you lose the knowledge about it.

Recently, a senior friend of mine who is an expert in financial management, Mr. Stephen Emasu, told me something that hit me again: "When you quit gainful employment, your income earning will drastically drop." He demonstrated by showing how the income falls along the X-Y axis. When we ended the meeting at the Protea Hotel in Kampala, I told myself I need to learn more about financial planning and management. My personal decision is now based on the formula that I have presented in the chapter. I need to learn more to become a better financial manager. I used to have a bad attitude only focusing on goals, personal vision and neglecting the economic aspects of my projects, but my spouse warned me never to trust people with money. It was good and true advice.

One day, I demanded an employee in our organization to give me weekly reports, but the employee sent in something that deviated from what we had agreed. When I did ask, do you know what happened? The employee went bazaar or acted angry with me, threatening even to quit the job. So many questions ran through my mind such as: If you are doing the right things with organization's money, then why would you get mad when I demanded reports and raised issues about the reports? I realized that what my spouse told me was true: Never trust people with money because they get tempted to cheat or misuse it. Now, I demand accountability for everything. I have no right to neglect any financial aspect of the business, so I take care of all activities. I resolve that I will pay attention to financial management with discipline.

However, I also have some additional issues to raise about financial management:

1. Work hard to earn money but be disciplined to manage it.
2. Develop good relationships with financial advisors just as you would develop relationships with lawyers or attorneys on legal matters.
3. Learn from others and use the knowledge to become better at financial management.
4. Read books on the topic of financial management.
5. Make financial management a personal business or responsibility.
6. Live a modest life and do not try to buy the whole "world."
7. Earn your money as you can, but manage your finances daily.

8. Never spend money you do not have and use money for investments, not leisure.

9. Save money for leisure or holidays, but these must not become a monthly thing to do.

10. Remember, always the truth or facts about money, including this one: "Resources are scarce."

Chapter 13

PRIORITIES

*Our life is the sum total of all the decisions we make every day,
and those decisions are determined by our priorities.*
−Myles Munroe

What Are Your Priorities In Life?

Truly, speaking I believe that having priorities in life is vital for successful, meaningful and impactful life. Where do you get your priorities? How do you decide on your priorities? There are millions of people who impulsively take on things or activities that are outside of their priorities. I know of people whose priorities are not defined. They make decisions based on what is urgent or their impulses. They are taken by what groups or friends invite them to do. For instance, they can be requested to join some parties or celebrations even if they have some things that are a priority; they abandon it and follow the group. I also discovered that our habits determine our priorities. Habits control everything that happens and they also influence our attitudes. Our attitudes are a product of our beliefs. Our beliefs can affect us positively or negatively, but in the end, they determine where we are destined in life.

There are many intelligent, smart and bright people in the world. They have great opportunities. They have tremendous potential. They have excellent skills, ideas, talents and resources at their disposal, but their priorities are skewed. I know a bright and intelligent person right who was an A+ student from the time he was a young pupil in a local school. I shall call Tolbert Dekker to conceal the identity. He always came as the best student in his class. He received all the opportunities that were available to him, including a supportive family and environment. He was not disadvantaged like some other people. The guy was naturally intelligent in class.

Tolbert Dekker was an up-and-coming young man with unlimited potential when he was in high school, but unfortunately, he misplaced his priorities in life. One of his top priorities appeared to be drinking in bars or clubs. He simply cannot stop the habit. As soon as the sun rises, he is thinking about where to find alcohol or any potent local brew. Because of misplaced priorities in his life, he is not living the life that most people expected out of him. In my opinion, he has destroyed his life. Each time I come across him, he is my teacher about life. Suppose his priorities were right, I believe I would not be writing this story in the book. I believe in your city, community, society or even country, there are people who are precisely like Tolbert Dekker.

〰〰〰〰〰〰〰〰〰〰〰〰〰〰〰〰〰〰〰〰〰〰〰〰〰〰〰〰〰〰〰〰〰〰

Priorities are a key
to focus and discipline.

〰〰〰〰〰〰〰〰〰〰〰〰〰〰〰〰〰〰〰〰〰〰〰〰〰〰〰〰〰〰〰〰〰〰

Why Are Priorities Important?

Lee Iacocca says, "To succeed today, you have to set priorities; decide what you stand for."[42] I like this quote because I believe it carries much wisdom. That wisdom gets into someone's mind; they can begin to progress in life. I do not know the person named Lee Iacocca, but I take the ideas he offers because they have great wisdom. As I was writing this book, I was thinking of Greek philosophers (thinkers like Plato, Socrates' and many others) who propagated their ideas, and millions of people in the world continue to believe those ideas. Do you know those Greek thinkers? For me, I have no idea of what these Greek thinkers even looked like or who they were apart from reading their views. A quote from Scott Caan says, "Good things happen when you get your priorities straight."[43] How many of us want good things? I believe if you asked that question to a large congregation of people in a mosque, church, college or any gathering, you would notice or count many hands raised within seconds.

What if you asked the question, "How many want bad things to happen?" Nobody will raise his or her hands up. People never wish bad things in life. Everyone wants good things. Everyone wants to be successful in any area. I guess the point to carry away is that priorities are a key to focus and discipline. When you understand your priorities, your life becomes simple and focused. However, the reverse is also true; if you never know and

42   https://www.azquotes.com/author/7129-Lee_Iacocca
43   https://www.brainyquote.com/authors/scott_caan

understand your priorities, you will be confused, divergent and scattered. It becomes difficult to go after your priorities. Priorities are essential:

Time is lost when priorities are unknown and undefined.

The greatest gift that God gave man is time. It is one of the most critical commodities or resources. There are many teachings available about time. In my book, Success Principles: Proven Secrets for Achieving Your Dreams and Vision, there is a whole chapter on time. How do you spend your time? When you spend your time, you either profit or lose. Most people are more focused on how they spend their money than how they spend their time. When money is lost, it can be regained or obtained. However, when time is lost, it cannot be recovered. The priorities that you now set and define determine how your time will be spent. Time will never be enough. Therefore, remember that time is a precious gift and it is priceless.

Time is a precious gift
and it is priceless.

Time cannot be changed, but our priorities can be adjusted.

Sometimes you hear people say, "I still need more time." Every day has 24 hours or 1,440 minutes. That means everyone has the same amount of time. Nobody has more time than others do. The billionaires and beggars have the same quantity. It does not matter what you say about time, but when you lose time, you cannot recover it. However, when you lose money, you have the chance to work and be paid or receive a gift. If 24 hours of today pass away when you have not done anything productive, you will not get those hours back. You will have to start waiting for tomorrow.

How do you manage time? Again, so many motivational experts on time have suggested several approaches to time management. They have given several ideas on this subject. However, I have a question about management: Can time be managed?

Nobody Can Do Everything

Many people are naïve in that they believe they can do all things. I was like that when I was in my 20s and 30s, but I learned that I could not do everything when I read the advice of Paul to the Philippians. Apostle Paul said, "Brothers and sisters, I do not consider myself yet to have taken hold of it. However, one thing I do: Forgetting what is behind and straining toward what is ahead, I press on toward the goal to win the prize for which God has called me heavenward in Christ Jesus."[44] Paul said one thing he could not forget what lies behind him (past); instead, he had to focus on to the goal and win a prize that God has prepared for him in heaven. Every person must get to a point when they do only one thing. Doing one thing makes life simple.

Instead of using your energy, time and resources to try to do so much, it is wise and reasonable to concentrate on one thing, or at most, two. Chinese author and philosopher Lin Yutang noted, "Besides the noble art of getting things done, there is a noble art of leaving things undone. The wisdom of life consists of elimination of nonessentials." It is always a good practice to get things done, but eliminating the trivial stuff is better. You can have anything you want, but you cannot have everything you want. My friend, Seth Tetteh from Ghana, said, "You cannot do everything. If you try to do everything, then everything will do you." A mature person's measure of maturity is determined by his or her knowledge of what he or she can and cannot do. You are not mature if you still believe you can do everything. You are also immature if you think you can do everything and have everything.

---

44   Philippians 3:13-14

◇◇◇

You can have anything you want,
but you cannot have everything you want.

◇◇◇

I believe the cause of depression, misery and stress in life for most people comes from that last part of the sentence. Many people want everything. What is everything? The only way to avoid this approach to life is making choices and decisions. Every person must choose what he or she wants. To get what you want, then you must do the right things rightly with excellence. You just have to let go of the rest of the other stuff. However, the challenge is also not having the capacity to know the right things. Do you do the right things? The right things are those things that are beneficial to you and not costly. If you have no idea of the right things, you can also imagine that you have only six months to be alive. What are those things that you need to do in those six months? The things that you do in a shorter time are the right ones. You need to write them down. You need to read and review each day until all those things get done.

Priorities help us change and choose life.

Whatever you become in life is a result of your choices and decisions. Whatever you are doing now is something you have decided to do. You want your priorities every moment every day. Some people never accept this fact. If you are still a teenager, there are chances that you are directed on what to do. However, if you are an independent adult, then you are responsible for your choices and decisions. You are the start of your life. You are the one who is responsible for the construction or destruction of your life. People make their life; they make decisions. To change your life, you need to decide and change your priorities.

◇◇

To change your life, you need to decide and change your priorities.

◇◇

We spend our time based on our priorities

Everything that a person does is done because of what a person chooses as his or her priorities. So, whatever is done is a person's choice. Some people do not believe that is true, but the reality is that the outcomes of life come from daily priorities. To become a competent person, there must be clarity of priorities and the simple way to have that is through goal setting. If priorities are established as goals, then it provides focus to the person. The reason why goals are not achieved is that people spend their time doing secondary or minor things. Priorities are like major things. To achieve excellent results, the focus must be on significant things. However, most people always have their attention on small things.

Furthermore, small things take away focus from significant things. There will always be many things that demand our attention. In the process, once our attention is diverted, the capacity to concentrate diminishes, and hence, the goals are never achieved. To have a higher concentration level, there is need to have focus. The key to success is having concentration, focus and running on your track. I learned about the concept of focus when I read a paragraph about the work written by an Italian economist, Vilfredo Pareto. Parento developed a rule or a formula for focus known as Parento principle that is applicable in life for any situation.[45] The Parento principle

45   https://en.wikipedia.org/wiki/Pareto_principle

states that by focusing your attention on the top 20 percent of all your priorities, you will be able to achieve 80 percent on your effort. Ever since I learned about the 20/80 rule, I keep applying it in my work. For instance, I can spend 20 percent of 24 hours to work to get 80 percent results. This principle has kept me on the track on doing more major things than minor things.

Many people want to change their lives. They have no idea how to do it. The primary reason why they are unable to change is because habits hold them. Habits are difficult to change and any changes requires time. One approach that I figured out was to decide on my priorities. Every day, I have goals on which I need to work. I decided that will take charge of my life by using every day effectively. Have you ever noticed that people who have nothing to do usually want to spend their time with you? Have you ever seen people who are going nowhere want to go with you? If you allow people like this to spend time with you, then you are wasting or spending away your life. Your time must be used effectively to work on your dreams. Free time must be used to rest, recover or recharge from accomplishing your tasks.

The poet Carl Sandburg said, "Time is the most valuable coin in your life. You and you alone will determine how that coin will be spent. Be careful that you do not let other people spend it for you."[46] The greatest valuable resource you have for changing your life is time. Every day, every person receives 24 hours, but how each person spends that resource is up to him or her. In today's world, people are affected or distracted by social media. People today also are distracted by e-mails, text messages and other interruptions. Others are preoccupied with unimportant tasks. They never take responsibility for how they spend their time. To take control of

---

the things and own your time, you must have a plan. My book, *Strategic Planning: Understanding the 3P's—Power, Purpose, and Process,* has ideas and simple steps for developing a plan. Apart from that, you also need to think through these questions and determine the answers yourself:

- What are your priorities in life?
- What must you do to bring out your priorities?
- What are you required to do?
- What gives you a most significant return, reward or benefit?

When you have answered those questions, then you have your priorities into clarity and focus. That means you have chosen significant things and discarded what is not essential or that needs to be overlooked. Philosopher William James said, "The art of being wise is the art of knowing what to overlook."[47]

Focus And Stay In Your Strength Zone

Every person has strength and weaknesses. Avoid focusing on your weaknesses. Always focus on your strengths. Whatever you want, you need to be persistent. The story of the persistent woman who wanted a judge to grant justice and another story of the man who wanted bread from a neighbor illustrate the need for persistence. Everything you want to do will not happen quickly. You must be focused and persistent. Never allow problems to stop you. You must endure. If you are persistent, you gain. How do you discover your strengths? Here are some ways:

1. **Trial and error.** You must try things in life and make mistakes. Through trial and error, you will gain insight into what works. Success and failure are the most excellent teachers ever. When you try things, you are likely to make mistakes. Those mistakes,

---

47   https://www.brainyquote.com/quotes/william_james_108497

however, make you learn.

2. **Seek feedback or counsel from others.** You can ask your family or closest friends to evaluate you to help you learn your strengths and weakness. It is not always comfortable to ask for feedback, but it helps you know your blind spots. Be careful to select those people without hidden motives or else they will not offer honest feedback or appraisal. If you have a mentor, you can ask the mentor's advice or assessment.

3. **Take a personal test.** Self-assessments using personality tests such as the DISC, Florence Littauer's Personality Plus and the Myers-Briggs Type Indicator can be very helpful.

4. **Learn from personal experiences.** You heard the statement that experience is the best teacher. Use your own experience to evaluate your strengths.

How To Manage Your Priorities?

There are so many things that are competing against time. Moreover, time is a resource that cannot be replaced. Money can be replaced or recovered, but time will never be replaced. The five actions you need to manage priorities are as follows:

1. **Evaluate your priorities daily.** You will need to create a system in which you review your priorities consistently. The need for change comes because of changes in conditions, situations and circumstances. Remember that your values must remain stable without changing. However, your priorities might require some degree of flexibility.

2. **Plan how to use your time carefully.** One of the things I have

done over the years is developing plans. I have a plan for 20+ years as well as what I should be doing in the next five years. Out of the long-term plans, I have also created short-term plans. Every day I know what I am supposed to be doing per my plans. However, most people never know what they are expected to do daily. They start their day without a plan. It is like a football team going to play a major competition without a plan. How can you expect to win or profit? It becomes difficult to get desired results. Everything that needs to be done daily must be written down. These things must be the major or important things based on 20/80 rule.

3. **Follow your plan and avoid distractions.** I have experience working in an environment where e-mail is the first thing you need to check on arrival to the office. Checking e-mails immediately takes you off the main plan. Some people start their day by reviewing newspapers or online papers. Again, these things take people away from the core tasks. I have witnessed that most managers or executives start working on major tasks midday or sometimes late afternoon. By that time, the law of diminishing return has begun. Significant things must be given attention. The most important task takes priority over the least important tasks or priorities.

4. **Delegate to your team as much as possible.** If you have a group of that works with you, you are safer delegating some responsibilities to others. Then, you wait to hold the person accountable for results delivered. There are two types of people in organizations: those who are perfectionists and those who are not. The perfectionist always wants everything submitted with absolute excellence. I learned about the concept of "delegation" from a management skills course

and then practiced it at my workplace. I gained a lot as it enabled me to focus on strategic tasks while my team members focused on tasks that could take a lot my time. The big challenge when it comes to delegation is deciding what tasks to give way. Some people "dump" responsibilities to others while others never delegate. They want to cling to tasks and do everything. The problem with clingers is they never get things done or moving. Those who dump their work (dumpers) often try to get rid of the tasks before them quickly and usually never think much about the tasks.

5. **Decide to invest in the right people.** To effectively have the right priorities, you need to learn to apportion time. How much time do you spend with people? Some people dwell on problems and those who are seeking solutions, people who are driven by feelings instead of passion, motives, goals and purpose. It is important to know that your associations determine where you will end. If you are not careful, you will waste time with people who are going nowhere and they normally want to go with you. If you are going to be effective, you need to have respect for everyone, but assess the value of the relationship, opportunities you will gain, insights, wisdom, inspiration or knowledge. Also, assess if they will be helpful in you getting to your destination, dream or vision. For me, I learned to spend time with only those who help me get to my vision. So, I invest my time in meaningful relationships, and several years ago, I decided to cut off some relationships.

A Review of My Priorities

I am thankful for learning to prioritize my life when I was still young man. The knowledge of prioritizing was further drilled into me when I started to work. My first workshop was organized at Lweza Conference Center in Kampala by Compassion International. I recall the facilitators emphasizing planning and prioritizing. I had gotten my first job as Project Director for Busiula Child Development Centre. Moreover, as a project director, I was expected to plan and set priorities against many needs.

- In my early teenage years, my priorities protected me from destroying my life through bad behavior and habits.

- In my 20s, my priorities supported my siblings in getting an education as well as helping me acquire knowledge, skills and the right attitude.

- In my 30s, my priorities were seeking knowledge about my passion, purpose and potential.

- In my 40s, my priorities have guided me to focus on improvement and making a difference.

- In my 50s, my priorities will help expand and grow my leadership to serve humanity.

Chapter 14

RELATIONSHIPS

A good relationship is one where someone accepts your pasts,
supports your present and encourages your future.
— Anonymous

No Human being Is An Island Or Mountain

I recently read a story of a woman who lived alone for 103 years. She lived without a man in her life. Her secret to a longer life at age 106 was, "No men, no stress." I asked my Rwandan friend, Richard Gatete, about his thoughts on this woman. His response was that was no life at all. I am convicted that human is designed to live with people; that is one reason the Lord God said, "It is not good for man to be alone, I will make a suitable helper for him."[48] What honestly happens when we have relationships?

You might have your views about these things. I have a single point

Genesis 2:28.

that I want to share with you as one who values relationships. To me, relationships are a source of and give meaning and fulfillment in life. No human on Earth can have meaning and fulfillment without relationships.

Relationships Are a Source of Meaning and Fulfillment in Life.

Do you agree? You can achieve everything you want in life, acquire higher education, make as much money as you want or accumulate all the wealth, power, popularity and fame you desire, but without good relationships, you will be an empty shell walking on the planet. There are thousands of people who are affected because they have no relationships with others. They have power and wealth but are living miserable lives.

Two Types Of People In The World

Our world is full of good and wrong people. The good people always have healthy relationships. The wrong people have weak or bad relationships. The good people are always concerned with human relationships. They have an awareness of the importance of people whereas the wrong people are never mindful or bothered about relationships. The wrong people are often greedy and deceptive. They never value people. They have behind their actions, "The end justifies the means." They also use people as objects, and when they have achieved their goals or plans, they throw them away as "rubbish." In other words, they trash them after using them.

The common characteristic of wrong folks is they never care of relationships. They always destroy bridges and never mind building the relationships. They also alienate others for their gains or interests. Do you have examples of such people in your community or neighborhood? I am sure you do. Recently, I was intrigued when a friend wanted to contest for local elections in my country. This person wished for my material and financial support to the campaign for an election. One of my closest friends said to me, "Do not waste your time and resources to support the guy because he will never win." Did I even ask why? I was informed that the candidate destroyed all bridges or relationships with everyone in that community. Nobody trusts him. I thought about this statement for two weeks. My conclusion was that trust is a key or foundation for successful relationships and leadership. It means people cannot lead others unless they have trustful relationships with those they lead.

Trust is a key or foundation for successful relationship and leadership.

One of the lessons I kept in my heart is that nobody can buy or pay for trust. Trust is earned through consistent behaviors and actions. It is easy to bribe or confuse people, but sooner or later, the truth will come out. Some people cover up their true character through humanitarian actions or helping the least in our society.

The Benefits Of Relationships With Other People

Have you ever tried to think of the crucial value of relationships? There are many benefits that relationship brings to people if they consistently decide to keep them. Here are some of the benefits I have discovered:

1. **Relationships provide significant experiences in life.** When I think about teamwork in all organizations, that I have worked with, I noticed that teams are built when there are trust and relationships among individuals. No single individual can claim to have achieved something alone without the support from others. Working with

others requires a great deal of focus on relationships. At a personal level, you will also realize that any significant experience or bright moment occurs when other people are involved. Every heart melts when people appreciate the contribution they have made. Every mind is changed when they know they have contributed. It is impossible to have great experiences or great moments when others are not involved. I want you to think about the bright moments of life in which people were not involved. You might find, there isn't any. The most significant experiences, victories and celebrations (including difficult moments) occur when people are participating. The most significant moments or experiences in life are achieved when the relationship is stable. The best things in life on Earth are produced when people connect and build a stable relationship based on universal values. Most people, however, ignore the importance of building relationships or networking.

The best things in life on Earth are produced when people connect and build a stable relationship based on shared values.

2. **Relationships enable people to enjoy life.** To enjoy life on Earth, you must learn to like and love people, including your enemies. One of the toughest things to do is to love people who attack or hate you. It is human nature to aspire to be liked and loved. On the other hand, it is also human nature to dislike or hate others. People who enjoy life have a quality of loving or liking people with whom they associate. The only way to enjoy life is by liking and loving people. Life becomes meaningful if only you can learn to live and love people. If you want to attract pain and misery, then you can continue to ignore others.

3. **Relationships enable growth and prosperity.** I think of a good life as the one where there is growth and prosperity. If a person is not achieving these two things, then I consider that as a sad life. Are you growing? Can you grow and prosper without the support of others? I think it is impossible to grow or prosper without others. The only way to grow and prosper is by learning to love and like people as well as yourself. Many people are intelligent, educated and gifted, but never prosperous. Why is that? It is because they have no stable relationships. They are full of themselves. If prosperity is to be attained, then there is a need for sensitivity to the needs and interests of others. People need to be appreciated and pleased. When people are pleased, they will have healthy, stable relationships that naturally propels growth and prosperity as well as reduces tensions and conflicts.

Various Forms Of Relationships

There are five main types of relationships that exist among people and determine how people interact and relate towards each other.

1. **Surface relationships.** This is the most common type which never goes beyond the point of knowing names, home backgrounds and probably positions held. Lack of strong commitment among people often characterizes this relation type. The people involved have a passive approach to the relationship. If the relationship is maintained, then there are higher chances of other relations blossoming out of the social interactions. It can serve as a foundation for other better forms of socialization that gives rise to other friendships and relationships.

2. **Structured relationships.** This type occurs between supervisors and subordinates. A relationship is produced from daily interactions or formal places such as places of work, schools, offices and others. The relations might be due to the pursuit of common goals, activities and obligations. Once those obligations or common goals have been achieved, then parties can disengage and then return later to a surface relationship type or create others.

3. **Secure relationships.** This type of relationship emerges as people feel comfortable with each other. When they feel safety and security of the other, they begin to be open and share experiences and problems. These relationships also emerge because of consistent behavior and conduct. It also arises from the trust that is built over time. The relationship becomes secure as people learn to trust and test their friendships. People spend time together doing similar things and share universal values and beliefs.

4. **Symbiosis relationships.** Have you heard the saying, "Scratch my back and I will scratch your back"? The association exists because those involved have no choice but to coexist. In most cases, people are in a relationship for motives, and once those motives are achieved, they quit. I want to compare the symbiotic relationship that exists between a parasite and host. When a parasite is satisfied, it stops being attached or connected to the host. What kind of relation do you have?

5. **Solid relationships.** These are the most important type of relationship that exists among people. I believe it is higher than any other relationship type that I have described so far. This relationship is manifested when there is complete trust and confidentiality. These relationships are the ones that create a long-term relationship. The goal of any relationship must be to lead to trust and confidence.

Relationship Mishaps

Have you imagined what causes breakages in relationships? Relationships are supposed to grow into a long-term relationship. There are many reasons why this happens. Joseph F. Newton said, "People are lonely because they build walls instead of bridges."[49] To avoid breakages of relationships, one must learn to handle people with "kid gloves," softly with the issue barely fisted. Furthermore, breakages in relationships occur because of mistrust, nepotism, abuse and criticisms. In addition, when parties lose a common goal or vision, the probability of relationship failure increases. If there is something important to remember, then it is this: Relationship is a choice just like everything else in life is a choice.

◇◇◇

A relationship is a choice
just like everything else in life is a choice.

◇◇◇

Social or Relational Skills Development

Every person must personally take responsibility to develop relationship skills so that they have the capacity and ability to interact with others. If a person wants to enjoy a fruitful, prosperous and purposeful life, then they must work at their social or relational skills. You will never get ahead in life if your people skills are weak. A majority of the poor people on Earth have inadequate social skills. They often have difficulties associating with others. They get alienated. Here are some of the consequences of poor people skills:

- If people never like you, then they will always look for ways to hurt you.
- If they fail to hurt you, then they will never help you.

49   https://www.forbes.com/quotes/5651/

- If they try to help you, they have the hope of you failing.
- If they hope you cannot succeed, then any victories you make remain empty to them.
- If you have stable relationships, then you will also know yourself. You will discover who you are.
- Relationships not only define who we are, but also determine what we become in life.
- Your level of success and achievement is directly related to the fruitful relationships you have enjoyed.
- I know you love me and you can't hurt me.
- I know you can help me if I need help.
- I know if I succeed, you will celebrate with me.
- I know if I fail, it will affect you, too.

How much success and accomplishments did you enjoy with people who did not like you? I guess your answer is no different from my view: very little or limited. I recall a time in my life when I had to live with people who did not liked me. You know what happened? I stagnated and stopped growing. I had the potential, but it was never maximized. So, be careful of the people with whom you relate or associate.

People and Organizations

If you carefully study any successful organization world over, you will notice the level of success depends on the people it has employed. If the people in the organization fail to cultivate excellent relations, the chances are that it will never go far. It is the people in the organization that attracts others to like the organization's products. Success is attained through people. You can check out any church, sports team, company, party or organization; then you will notice that its success was dependent on its people. Jim Collins, author of From Good to Great, has written about the significance of recruiting of which he refers to as "getting the right people on the bus."[50] I believe this so right. You can bet me on this: All successful companies value the people they have recruited.

Get the right people on the bus.

Therefore, the critical point is always appreciating your people because they are the significant assets that you possess that determine how much value you gain as an organization. Remember that people are complicated but learn to manage them.

Establishing Solid Relationships

If you aspire to live a productive and influential life, this is one of the noble tasks. You will have to work to build stable relations with others. Nobody will do it for you. It will be your choice and decision to invest in stable relations. How do we develop stable relations? Most people have no clue about this. I recommend that you read a book by Dale Carnegie: How to Win Friends and Influence People. If there is any single investment in life worth doing, then it is opening "relationship bank accounts" to invest time and energy in the relationship.

You must choose what investments you want to make. One of them is an investment in relationships. It is a personal choice and responsibility. A lot of people never bother about investing in relationships. They expect relationships to happen on their own without any effort. A stable relationship is established on trust and transparent communication. Other ways to establish long-term and robust relation include the following:

50   Jim Collins, *Good to Great* (New York: Harper Business, 2001), 67.

- **Change your mind about people:** How do you deal with people who are different from you? It is a hard thing to do always, but as a human being, you need to adjust and know that nothing changes in life until your mind changes. The only way things are going to change is when you decide to change.

- **Make people so essential and worthy:** If you place people as the most important asset in your life, then you will never worry about the outcomes. If you decide to care about people, then establishing strong relationships have to become a top priority. However, if you learn to value people, then everybody is somebody. Learn to love people, not things. Love people but use things; never use people. People hate to be used. You must learn to expect people to do their best, but if it does not happen the way you expect, then learn to lower your expectations. If you expect too much from people, you are headed for disappointment. I learned years ago a lesson that has protected my life: The only way to minimize my disappointments is to lower my expectations of people.

- **Be friendly to everyone:** It will not cost you much to be friendly to people even though they are not your friends. Give people your friendship but never expect more from them. You must value them and know that they are made in God's image on Earth just as you are.

- **Be respectful:** You must give respect to people always, but never expect them to respect you. If you want respect, then you must work for it and get paid for it. When you get paid with respect, it implies you have earned it. That is why they say that respect is earned, not given. If you are respectful, then people will always respect you. They will never hurt you. You have heard the saying,

"You reap what you sow." This is a law on Earth that cannot be changed. To me, every person deserves to be respected because everyone has value. Nobody is useless. Every person was created for a purpose by God. No human being can create anything close to human beings. Respect cannot be demanded, but instead, it must be earned. How? You must learn to respect yourself, respect others and become valuable. Then, you will be paid back with respect by others. Then you earn it. That is why it is often said that respect is earned but never demanded.

- **Learn to understand people:** Understanding is one of the things about life that is crucial. Knowing and understanding can help you protect your life. You can protect your relationships if you can learn more about people. If you do not know people, then you will misunderstand them.

- **Make a personal commitment to add value to others:** If you can help people grow or become better, then it will be easy to relate to them. If you want to add value, then you must help people to know and identify their abilities and support others as they develop them. People today commonly enter relationships with expectations or wrong motives. As you add value, never expect returns. You also need to check your motives for being in a relationship. If you are in a relationship for evil motives, then it is not worth it. Finally, avoid the temptation to control or manipulate people. Just be honest and transparent in your relationship with them. If you have no common interest or values, you need to accept that simple fact and live your life.

- **Put people first before things:** I learned two things over the years: putting people first and being selfless. Some people are known for selfishness. If you are selfish, it is not easy to build a relationship; however, one of the golden rules of life is: Do unto others what you would want them to do unto you. Having this mindset opens doors of friendship with others and you will not go wrong. Remember to have a positive attitude, show people that they matter and that you are interested in their well-being. Another secret is being open and smiling at people, getting to know their names, and being willing to help. People do not care about how much you know until they know how much you care about them.

- **Always avoid carrying negative emotions:** The things that have brought you setbacks (pain, problems, miseries or your past experiences) must never be allowed to interfere with new relationships. Let the new relationships start afresh with brightness or a clean slate. For most people, however, they carry their emotional baggage as they start new associations. You cannot carry emotions and expect good relationships. Suppose you have been hurt in the past; you could not change that experience. There are two ways to deal with it: Either you forget about, or you live in misery forever in your life. It is your choice. You must learn to bury the past and move on. I know this is tough, but it must be done if you are going to maximize the benefits of a new relationship.

- **Make time for relationships:** If you want to enjoy friendships with others, you must decide to allocate time to be with people. Relationships become meaningful if only time is given to them. Your priority must be with the people that matter most in your life. Your family and close friends must get a share of your time and made to feel important. You should listen to their concerns, fears, worries, plans and opportunities. Help them by following the truth about people.

- **Be willing to serve others:** When you serve people, you will receive appreciation. You will receive recognition. Matthew 20:25-28 says:

Jesus called them together and said,

> *"You know that the rulers of the Gentiles lord it over them, and their high officials exercise authority over them. Not so with you. Instead, whoever wants to become great among you must be your servant, and whoever wants to be first must be your slave— just as the Son of Man did not come to be served, but to serve, and to give his life as a ransom for many."[51]*

<><><><><><><><><><><><><><><><><><><><><><><><><><><><><><><><><>

Serving others is not an easy task and requires humility.

<><><><><><><><><><><><><><><><><><><><><><><><><><><><><><><><><>

- **Learn to appreciate and love people:** Jesus said, "And the second is like it: Love your neighbor as yourself."[52] It is natural to dislike people, but one must remember to love and help people. If you show love, you will receive it back. If you show hate, then you will get the same measure. Learn to say thank you or appreciate the contribution of people in your life. Sometimes, they might disappoint you, but try to love them until perhaps when you fail. Besides, appreciating people leads to happiness. Happiness is essential in life. One of the rules of life is to be happy. Being happy without any regrets is a good thing.

---

51   Matthew 20: 25-28.
52   Matthew 22:39.

How To Understand People

Many people never really get to know others. The reasons are many. To understand people, you need to be present with them. You need to be in touch with them. Do not be distant with people. Never build walls but choose to extend a helping hand or build a bridge instead. Let people distance themselves from you, but always extend a helping hand. The truth about people is so important to remember. People have shortcomings... help them become better.

- People are insecure...help them become secure.
- People want to feel good...make them feel good.
- People want a better future...give them hope and faith.
- People want to be understood...learn to listen to them.
- People are greedy and selfish...you help them meet their needs.
- People get negative attitudes...inspire them to gain positive attitudes.
- People become emotionally low ...encourage them to become strong.
- People want to succeed... help them succeed.
- Not every person will like you... get used to this fact.

If you can master this truth, then the foundation for good relationships is established.

The Benefits of My Relationships

When I reflect on my relationships, some of them made me smile while others made me sad. The sad ones are the ones that pains me, but I tried my best. I was always patient with everyone I related to life. I think one of my greatest strengths is patience. If I give up on a relationship, it means I have tried my best. One day I was having an evening tea meeting with my relatives at Jokas Hotel near Nambole Stadium in Kampala. One of my younger brothers, Peter Alfred Okello, said; "Samuel has never beaten me in my entire life, and by the time you part company with Samuel, then it means he has tried to keep you close. The last thing Samuel will do is let you go forever." My relations were beneficial in the following ways:

- Relationships gave me inspiration and motivation.
- Relationships gave me life's insights, information and knowledge and wisdom.
- Relationships helped me discover myself.
- Relationship enabled me to grow and expand.
- Relationships provided me with wonderful experiences and memories.

When I think of the most rewarding relationships I have had, I know a couple of people whom wished me so well. They are Moses Ojota, Michael Omeke, Joseph Omoding, Leya Akampumuriza, Grace Amuron, Simon Anguria, and Brenda Piloya. I remember the great moments and memories. When I think about these people, I am reminded of so many times they stood by me against all the odds. These are what I call real friends. It has been a great privilege and honor to know them. If I must tell the stories of our relationship, I have much to write.

Toxic Relationship

This is the worst forms of relationships. Sometimes, relationships start on a sound footing, but with time, things change. You can find that people who were close in the beginning may have different interests, goals and values now. If they become toxic, the best option is to accept to take different directions and learn what caused the relationships to become sour or bad. I like to compare toxic relationships like "Sour milk when it gets bad." You have no choice, but to let go.

Chapter 15

VALUES

*A people that values its privileges
above its principles soon loses both.*
—Dwight D. Eisenhower

The Danger Of Ignoring And Abusing Values

It was a Wednesday afternoon. A friend and colleague of mine sent me a message. Dr. Athanasius Mutaawe Lubogo, who was an Epidemiologist with World Health Organization (WHO), told me about the appointment of another friend, Mr. Stephen Emasu, as a board member with UMEME, an electricity company in Uganda. Although I already knew three months before he sent the message, Stephen was excited about the appointment. It was the first time that Dr. Lubogo learned about the appointment. Stephen is a man with extensive knowledge and experience; he consults with World Bank and International Monetary Fund. Mr. Emasu has been a consultant and advisor for various governments: Rwanda, Kenya, Liberia, Namibia, Uganda and Somalia. He offers technical support in strengthening financial management systems for government's Ministry of Finance and Planning. He also served as a leader with Price Waterhouse Coopers in Uganda.

Later that afternoon, I met Dr. Lubogo at the dining hall; he brought the issue again up. He said shareholders of the company had rejected the appointed board member for UMEME. The shareholders rejected the nominee ("Paul," which is not his real name) as a board member because of his bad track record in which his name had been continuously associated with the loss of millions of shillings in Uganda. We discussed the issue and the message that was too clear was that the integrity of Paul had been questioned.

On the other hand, the shareholders did not doubt Mr. Emasu's integrity and credibility. Before that, there was also a similar incident in which one of the senior cabinet ministers, "Madam Paulina," (not her real name) appeared before a national commission of inquiry on land matters established by the President of Uganda. The minister was thoroughly exposed as she was accused of abuse of office and public funds, creating private companies and using federal funds for personal gain.

What do you think is wrong with Paul and Paulina in the story? To me, they have issues related to their ethics, morals and values. What do you think about the perceptions of their children when they witnessed or read in the papers about them? The information about the duo was on television and in the newspapers. The damage caused by ignoring and abusing values, morals, and ethics is profound. It hurts so badly. If people or leaders have no morals, ethics and values, then it affects many areas of their lives. In the case of Paul and Paulina, their images and credibility were tarnished entirely. It is a moral disaster if the person does not live according to morals, ethics and values. Dr. Lubogo said, "The should resign and go home." I agreed with his message. What is important to note is that every time an individual or leader violates principles and does not live according to decided morals, ethics and values, there will be damage to his or her character. In one of my books, *Excellent Character: A Principal Requirement for Successful Leadership,* I dedicated chapters on values. I debated internally about the necessity of writing a chapter on values in this book. My final decision was that it does not harm to include it here because some people might have access to one or both books from the bookstore.

The Long-Lasting Nature of Values

When I think of values, my simple conclusion is that values are longer-lasting than human beings. If you do not agree with this statement, let me prove to you what I am talking about. I have had an opportunity to work with large humanitarian organizations, and each of them has core values. For instance, World Vision is one of the most significant reliefs and advocacy organizations for children in the world. Dr. Bob Pierce founded it in the early 1950s. World Vision has existed for over 50 years. Another example is the United Nations formed after World War II. The values of these two organizations have outlasted all the initial members who founded them. Even the people presently working as employees will die, but the values will stay forever. Values outlast people. Values are therefore very powerful. One of the lessons you learn from that message is that values must never be changed. Values must be preserved and lived.

Examples of Values

When I think of values, I think about so much, and they serve as principles that govern the universe. Here are a few examples of values for your consideration:

- The value of love.

- The value of faithfulness.
- The value of maturity.
- The value of kindness.
- The value of integrity.
- The value of honesty.
- The value of discipline.
- The value of humility.
- The value of respect.
- The value of hard work.
- The value of obedience.
- The value of faith.
- The value of accountability.
- The value of sincerity.
- The value of steadfastness.
- The value of responsible living.
- The value of truthfulness.
- The value of commitment.
- The value of self-sacrifice.
- The value of compassion.
- The value of fairness.
- The value of justice.
- The value of laws.

The Crisis Of Losing Values

Across all the continents of the world, there are reports of immoral behavior and lost values. The media at any level have played a significant role in bringing out the things that nobody would ever come to know. The degree to which leaders at any level are falling is unimaginable. The values have been washed away like sand on the seashores. There are many forms of corruption, including sex scandals. There are several cases of abuse of humans and trafficking. There are many issues that are not even reported. Is it possible to avoid all these emerging problems because of decay in morals or values? Of course, it is possible.

What damage does an immoral decision and cause to followers? Estimating the pain or the magnitude is difficult. I believe that all the moral diseases can be prevented. When I was young, there was a common saying, "Prevention is better to cure." For some people, they only thing that you need to guard against is diseases. Ideally, that should be the case. But, other aspects of life must also be safeguarded. The need to prevent moral diseases is more crucial now. If moral diseases are not prevented, then so many tragedies will be experienced. The destiny of many people will be aborted or canceled prematurely. In every society, children are taught morals. Certain actions are taken to instill discipline, honesty and other values. I recall my dad always told us, "You must speak the truth always." That message got implanted into my soul and became like a deep root in my life.

Why Do Values Matter In A Person's Life?

You can think of several reasons. Before we dive to understand why values are significant, I will want to pose two questions. Do you want to finish well? Do you want a significant legacy? If your answer to those two questions is yes, then pursue the direction of values. Now, let's return to why values count; here are some thoughts:

1. **Values serve as a true north, giving accurate direction.** Life is a constant struggle between good and bad, good and evil, light and darkness. Life is about making choices and decisions. Life is about making changes and adopting new changes. Life is about managing situations and circumstances. Life is about handling challenges, problems, desires and managing expectations. The only way to navigate through life under all those changes is to allow values to become a guiding morning star or "The True North."

Regardless of any turmoil, change or circumstances, the true north direction will remain constant.

2. **Values prevent infection from "moral diseases."** If you work with health specialists or professionals, you often hear terms like "communicable diseases." Communicable diseases can be transmitted from one patient to another through association. For instance, you cannot get an Ebola unless you are exposed to patients with Ebola symptoms. If you have no contact with an Ebola patient, the chances are that you will be 100 percent sure of being alive. Most of the patients that die from communicable diseases acquire the virus. If the speed of transmission is high, what can you expect but many causalities. The same is true of values. If you get exposed to environments in which wrong values are displayed and applied, you will be infected and affected by the good virus that eventually leads to moral disease. If it is not treated or managed, the case will die. Doctors like calling it "case management," a term used to refer to the care, stabilization and treatment of patients until there is the full recovery.

3. **Values prevent individuals from early death.** Have you observed how people make decisions whenever there is a crisis, a problem or turmoil? Some people panic; others stay still. Some people react; others respond. I have been in a situation in which I am expected to decide when the times are rough or identify challenging moments. I learned that during those challenging moments, there is fear, anxiety, depression and many effects. Some people experience joy, peace and serenity even in times of rapid change. The only safety during rough moments is the application of values. Without values, it is impossible to survive the torrential storms or rains of life. Values, however, will offer you the way out or the direction.

Without values, anyone can drift slowly but eventually will be swallowed or killed by the moral disease. The torrential storms, waves and rains can cause destruction costing millions of dollars or pounds. I do not think anyone wants to go that direction, but most people do it either intentionally or without knowing it is happening. If you have strong values, they can be the supporting rod over troubled waters or when torrential speed intensifies.

4. **Values serve as an anchor in life.** As you saw what happened to Paul and Paulina, you realize that they made decisions and choices. Not all their decisions, however, were guided by values. I have listed values under its own chapter. If they had applied values to decide, then the outcomes would have been different. How do make decisions based on values? Some people find it hard to decide based on values. For example, if you are attempted to decide to steal public funds, you can ask the questions: Is my decision fair, just or honest; am I doing the right thing?

5. **Values are comparable to "A trusted friend."** How do you define a friend? I have a simple definition of a friend that I have applied to my life for over 15 years. A friend is anyone who supports me to achieve my vision with principles. There are many people with whom I interact daily; some of them are acquaintances or old friends. Some old friends may have changed their value systems. As you can see, acquaintances never really care about the vision you have.

The Most Intangible and Valuable Things

When I examined my own life as reflected in my container room in Chelsea Village in Somalia, I concluded that the I had intangible assets that have helped me in my life for many years. These intangibles are critical because they play an essential role in my journey on Earth. Here are some intangible things that have propelled my life up until the present days:

- My attitude.
- My priorities.
- My health.
- My family.
- My goals.
- My thoughts or ideas.
- My commitment.
- My finances.
- My relationships.
- My big-heartedness.
- My values or character.
- My faith.
- My growth or learning.

Through the various experiences in life and the search for the life's purpose and meaning, I was able to figure out my purpose on Earth. I believe I was born "To equip and empower aspiring leaders with resources, training and mentoring to serve humanity." That purpose is so critical. It guides my decisions. To fulfill that timeless purpose, I realized I needed to examine my values and intangible assets. I was again able to identify those values that will serve me as I pursue my purpose. The process of setting values is not easy, but the more you grow, encounter challenges, experiences and lessons, the easier it becomes to know what is valuable for you. My core values have now become more important than riches, jobs and wealth. No amount of money can attract me to lose my values. The values are implanted into my soul. When I was pursuing my doctorate, I studied a lot about values, culture, character and many other topics. I used that opportunity to reexamine my values and determine what is valuable to me. The following are the five most important things:

1. **My relationship with God, my Source.** Without God, everything becomes impossible.

2. **My family.** This is my greatest obligation: to protect, provide, teach, train, mentor and transfer my values to family.

3. **Myself.** Through my existence on Earth, I believe I will be able to continue serving God, my family and others.

4. **My purpose and work.** Through my purpose, I will make a difference in the world. Someone one day will benefit from my books, and they will write back to me that my ideas helped them.

5. **My friends.** My friends are willing to work with me and are committed to my vision and mission.

When I reflect on my journey, I sometimes cry and experience the pain of losing parents and relatives at a tender age. Those events taught me some of the things that my teachers or professors never taught me. For instance, my mother taught us about God: to have faith in God and trust God always. For most of my life, I pray silent prayers to my Spirit even when I am in meetings. I believe her teachings impacted my personal life.

What Is The Way Forward?

You might be thinking what's next? My message is simple. You need to become proactive in the way you want your journey on Earth to become. Your values and purpose must influence the direction of your life. From this moment onwards, you must make a personal decision that you will never again violate or ignore your values. If you do, you do that at your own personal peril. The price of violating values is higher than anything worth doing. List your values; keep them close to you, and every day, make decisions based on your values. The best decision you can ever make is a personal decision to live by your values, to embrace them and to practice every moment to stay within your values. Your values will eventually start to send messages outside. Then you will become a person known by your values.

Usually when people meet me who have known me, they say you are still the same person. Some years back, I used to imagine or think about what they meant by that. Later I was able to figure out what that statement meant. My interpretation of those interactions is this: "Continue to live according to your values; do not mess up or compromise anything with your values." There is one thing that is common to all people on Earth: You might not be watching yourself, but people are watching you every moment. How they see you is how they will take you. Their perception becomes a reality about you. Why? They do not see what you do in private. They do not know your inner, secret life, but your life is on display every day.

Another experience, I learned is that it is very difficult to change people. Personal change comes from revelation or transformation in the spirit of the mind. It comes from the renewing of the mind as Apostle Paul wrote in Romans 12:2. Values cannot be planted and have their benefits harvested in a short period. It takes years to grow values and apply them. People are not born with values but acquire them instead. People are born with gifts and talents. People learn skills and competencies. With their values, however, people identify them and then cultivate and protect them.

People are born with gifts and talents.
People learn skills and competencies.
With their values, however,
people identify them and then
cultivate and protect them.

Why Do People Have Regrets in Life?

When you have regret, it means there is something that you did and the consequences were grave, which impacted your life and your destiny. Everybody fails, makes mistakes and does not seem to achieve everything. That is okay. It is part of the game called life. However, if you are interested in finishing well and receive a crown of life from the Creator, then start today never to compromise on your values. If you compromise on your values, you will have many regrets. I learned to avoid regrets by making decisions based on my values and studying the consequences before deciding on anything. It is easy to decide, but living with regrets is painful. I have personal experience on this, and I have paid the price on my carelessness.

I learned to avoid regrets
by making decisions based on my values
and studying the consequences
before deciding on anything.

There is also something I want to share with you. If you examine successful organizations, you will notice that the organization's values are more important than the people. Do you agree? I know you doubt me. Let me share an experience. There was a top official of the United Nations who worked in one of the Federal States in South Sudan. This guy was powerful and held a top official with a lot of access to power and opportunities. The guy "illegally imported" a woman from another country in West Africa to South Sudan for about two weeks. He did everything well, but then the secret was discovered. The guy had ignored or abused the values of the UN. This guy was sent away after the investigators established that he had not kept the core values at his workplace. When you are a manager in an organization, there is always some truth in the fact that human resources are the most important resource than anything. This is not 100 percent true. There are other intangible assets, such as goodwill or the image of the organization. Every organization will work hard to protect its name. They do that by keeping their core values.

How Do You Avoid Regrets In Life?

I will make some suggestions without expounding on what you need to do as follows:

1. Make a list of your core values.
2. Know your values by heart.
3. Decide to live your life based on your core values always.
4. Make sure people around your circles know your core values.
5. Teach your values to your family and workers.
6. Every day compare your decisions with your values.
7. Live according to your values, not emotions.
8. Evaluate or assess how you are performing about your values.

How To Change Or Transform One's Life

I have always asked myself how to change or transform my life. Most times, I meet people who should review their lives and change them. I was sharing with my Zimbabwean friend, Claudel on this question one mid-morning in a coffee shop. I left that shop and thought about how change can occur. Here are some ways to change:

1. **Decide to change.** Life only changes when you decide to change, establish your core values and live by them.

2. **Become a person of high value.** Albert Einstein said, *"Try not to become men of success. Rather become men of value."*[53] Is this simple? Yes. Work on your character and your worth will go up. Worth is the same as value.

3. **Review and reflect on the values that you live constantly.** What do you value? You realize the impact that changes your entire life dramatically.

4. **Decide based on your values, not emotions.** Always control and manage emotions in life.

Values Are A Source Of Character

In my book, *Excellent Character: A Principal Requirement for Successful Leadership*, I have extensively written about character. When you think about character, it is a concept that has been misinterpreted. We have two types of character: good and bad. How character is formed has also been carefully presented. In this work, I do not want to go back to what is already presented in that book. I want to draw to your attention a statement that I believe is critical: Character is the foundation of leadership. Leadership is one thing that is critical in every area (for example, community, society, organizations or nations), but leadership has been misunderstood. Leaders

---

are needed for many reasons, which you can read in my other book, *Becoming an Influential Leader: How to Gain and Sustain it with Others in Your generation.*

For most people, when they hear the concept of a great leader or leadership, they immediately think of big names like Donald Trump, Barack Obama, etc. Those people have been given great responsibility to lead their countries, states or organizations. The truth is, however, that anyone can be a great leader. Anyone who masters the art of influencing others is a leader. We must be careful; however, there is a difference between manipulating and inspiring. True leaders inspire people to follow them while deceptive leaders survive through manipulating their followers.

Anyone who masters the art of influencing others can become a leader.

Leading people is simply having the capacity to influence them and change their thought patterns, beliefs and actions to achieve common goals. Leading also means being willing to work with people always to make a difference. There are so many things that leaders enjoy: both success and failure as well as gain and pain. To become a leader, however, requires the development of character, skills and knowledge among other traits. Character is a core requirement or principle for becoming a leader. A person of character is more trusted than a person with bad character. Leaders think of the future; they imagine a better future. They take people from the known to the unknown. They bring the best out of people. They transform their followers' thoughts.

In my studies and experience, I have noted that true leaders are reluctant and hate power or popularity. They love to be by themselves. They are never selfish. For instance, Moses argued with God about leading the Israelites. He had requested God to appoint another person. He knew his limitations, and because of that, he was saying to God, "Get someone else." If you see people pursuing leadership positions, however, their interests are not about making a difference and could actually be other motives.

True leaders also sacrifice themselves for the sake of their vision. They are not full of themselves. Instead, they have self-discipline that comes from a clear sense of purpose (or knowing what a leader is expected to do) and meaning for life. Vision is seeing what a leader is expected to do. A true leader has knowledge of their purpose and a clear vision of their destiny.

Some other characteristics of leaders include:

- True leaders are strong but never rude.
- True leaders are kind but never weak.
- True leaders are bold but are never bully.
- True leaders are thoughtful but not lazy.
- True leaders are humble but never timid.
- True leaders are proud but never arrogant.
- True leaders learn from others but never become like them.
- True leaders empower others but never manipulate them.

The Integrity Test

All true leaders must have unquestionable integrity. If a leader's integrity comes under scrutiny, then the leader's values were not loud enough to protect the leader. A leader must uphold their values and principles at all times to protect themselves from the maladies of bad character or infections that affect character. The character of a leader is constantly being tempted or tested by his actions and responses to followers or other leaders. The only way a leader-follower relationship is built and sustained is by maintaining trust. Nobody will follow a leader if he or she do not have trust in that leader. In other words, influence is possible only if followers have trust in their leader. It is important to have a self-evaluation of your life and decide to live an honest life. Your integrity must never come under question.

Furthermore, true leaders practice what they say. Their words, actions and thoughts are the same. True leaders are optimistic rather than pessimistic. True leaders know their destination. They know where they are going. They even show people where they are heading going and inspire them that destination is better than their current location. People follow leaders who know where they are.

Where are you going? As a leader, you must know where you are going. A great leader is optimistic of the future because they have a vision that pulls them through all kinds of difficulties, problems or challenges. A true leader not only knows where they are, but also know how to get to a preferred future. Here are some ways true leaders influence followers:

- Create a positive vision of the future.
- Develop a plan to gets to the future.
- Communicate the vision and plan.
- Work on the plan.
- Identify a team to support in plan implementation.

Why Does Character Matter in Life?

The answers to that question are available with my own views about character being found in my book entitled, *Excellent Character: A Principal Requirement for Successful Leadership.* Instead of giving the reasons, I humbly encourage you to read that work.

EPILOGUE

God knows our situation;
He will not judge us as if we had no difficulties to overcome.
What matters is the sincerity and perseverance
of our will to overcome them.
– C. S. Lewis.

What Do You Consider As Pillars Of Your Life?

All leaders and people need to study the pillars described in this book. The reason I recommend all people to read this book is that it will help them understand what matters each day in their lives. You might have so many ideas about what matters, but these ideas are what I have concluded as critical in life after several years of research and traveling to different contexts. Why use the word pillars? The answer is simple: The strengths of a building structure depends on the pillar. A pillar is the upright and firm support of a superstructure. A life of a person can be viewed as a superstructure standing on the firm and upright support. When pillars are weak, the superstructure is bound to collapse. Please read this book repeatedly until it gets into your spirit.

This book is what I consider as life's handbook. A handbook is what you refer when you get confused or perplexed on crucial matters of life. This book has lots of great ideas and those ideas transform lives. If you practice these ideas, you will become in charge of your life. You need to decide to understand what matters. If you decide, then that decision is a good one. Remember this truth: Good decisions will lead to a good life. A good life is produced by good decisions today. Good decisions lead to a better tomorrow. Some people never think of the fact that a good decision today will give you a better tomorrow. The lack or absence of success in many people's lives is a product of poor decisions they made. The poor decisions and choices normally lead to negative consequences, bad experiences and memories. They keep wondering why they are not getting ahead in life.

However, making good decisions is not as simple as it seems. Still, they must be made because they are necessary for success. Your decision to read this book is a good one, too. Let me share a crucial point in decision-making that has helped me. Theodore Hesburgh, former president of Notre Dame University, said, "You don't make decisions because they're easy. You do not make decisions because they're cheap. You do not make decisions because they're popular; you make decisions because they're right."

There is a saying: "All authors have so much to write." That is true. However, time and resources are limited. Let me also say something about discipline. A good life comes from discipline and good decisions. If you have a desire for a good life, then you must learn the art and science of making good decisions and living a disciplined life. Before you make any decisions, you must evaluate the consequences. When you make good decisions, then you must also practice discipline every day. The first raw material for success is making good decisions, but when you add self-discipline, you will experience the different taste of life. Let me get practical here. Most people want to be thin and lightweight, but check their plates of food during meals. Most people want to succeed, but check their commitments, values, decisions, ideas, thinking, attitudes and relationships. Most people want to be rich, but they are not willing to do what is right. People always want an easy life. They do not want to work hard.

When you think about life deeply, then you realize that success is not an accident. It comes because of pain. People successfully overcome their feelings and fears to form habits of doing things that unsuccessful people never like to do at all. There are two things that I want to leave you: decisions and disciplines. Decisions will help you start, but discipline will help you finish what you start. Most people want to avoid pain. Remember, discipline is often painful. We need to remember that there are two kinds of pain: the pain of discipline and the pain of regret. A majority of people avoid the pain of discipline because it is always an easy thing to do. What they do not know is that the pain of self-discipline is beneficial whereas the pain of regret is long lasting.

Finally, if we constantly compromise or neglect our discipline, then the rewards, benefits and opportunities significantly decrease. Likewise, the probability of failure increases. Regrets will grow in high proportions. However, when we decide to subject ourselves to the pain of discipline, rewards and benefits are great; our opportunities increase. The probability of success also increases.

SALVATION
PRAYER

What is the sinner's prayer? Why does a sinner need salvation? Why should a sinner take the salvation prayer? The sinner's prayer (or salvation prayer) is a Christian term for a prayer that is said when people want to repent of their sins, ask God for forgiveness and state their beliefs in the life, death and saving resurrection of Jesus Christ. Paul wrote,

> *If you declare with your mouth, "Jesus is Lord," and believe in your heart that God raised him from the dead, you will be saved. For it is with your heart that you believe and are justified, and it is with your mouth that you profess your faith and are saved.*[54]

Millions have come to a saving relationship with Jesus Christ through family, friends and church services leading them in the salvation prayer. The words in the prayer do not save. Jesus Christ alone has the power to save through faith. Let me explain something about the salvation prayer. It's not the prayer that saves; it's the repentance and faith behind the prayer that lays hold of salvation. The salvation prayer can help you communicate to God

---

54   Romans 10:9-10.

that you have repented of your sins, have accepted His forgiveness and have accepted Jesus Christ as your Lord and Savior.

The Sinner's or Salvation Prayer

> *Lord Jesus, for too long I have kept you out of my life. I know that I am a sinner and that I cannot save myself. No longer will I close the door when I hear you knocking. By faith, I gratefully receive your gift of salvation. I am ready to trust you as my Lord and Savior. Thank you, Lord Jesus, for coming to Earth. I believe you are the Son of God who died on the cross for my sins and rose from the dead on the third day. Thank you for bearing my sins and giving me the gift of eternal life. I believe your words are true. Come into my heart, Lord Jesus, and be my Savior. Amen.*

If you have prayed this prayer in sincere faith, you may want to put your initials by the prayer along with today's date as a reminder that you have come to Christ in faith, trusting Him as your Lord and Savior. If you have sincerely prayed that prayer, please write to me using the following address and share your commitment with me.

Another thing is that you might be interested is our training, coaching, mentoring, seminars and workshops in the areas of leadership, character development, planning, understanding and pursuing purpose, overcoming crises, maximizing potential and developing and pursing vision among many other areas. If you are interested in any of the above, do contact me through the means provided here.

Dr. Samuel Odeke, DSL
C/O CTSL Uganda

P.O. Box 34820 Kampala, Uganda
P.O. Box 2648 Mbale, Uganda
Telephone: +256783563417/782276765
E-mail: samuel.odeke@yahoo.com
Website: www.samuelodeke.com

ABOUT THE AUTHOR

Dr. Samuel Odeke was born in poor family and neighborhood in Bukedea in Eastern Uganda. He is the firstborn of a family of ten children from three mothers. His parents served as civil servants and as peasant farmers. Dr. Odeke's story is one of rising from humble beginnings and flowing to the top. He believes anybody can overcome any challenges provided they are willing to learn, persist, work hard and believe God. He is married with three children. Dr. Odeke experienced tragedy when he lost his mother at age 14, his grandfather at 15 and his grandmother at 18. Those traumatic events and experiences changed his perception of life. As a result, he began to search for answers related to life. As a teenager, Dr. Odeke also witnessed the impact of war, conflict and massive cattle raids in his district of Bukedea (formerly part of Kumi District) in the late 1980s, where hundreds of lives and properties were lost. Many times, he survived death from both government soldiers and rebels. He attended rural primary schools before joining high school and Makerere University later.

Dr. Odeke received a Bachelor of Science Degree and Post Graduate Diploma in Education from Makerere University. In addition, he received an M.A. in Organizational Leadership and Management from Uganda Christian University. He also holds a Post Graduate Diploma in Public Administration and Management as well as a Master of Management with Specialization in Public Administration and Management from Uganda Management Institute. Dr. Odeke earned a Doctor of Strategic Leadership with a specialization in Strategic Leadership from Regent University in 2017.

Dr. Odeke has worked for over 15 years with large humanitarian and development organizations such as World Vision, United Nations World Food Programme (WFP), United Nations Children's Fund (UNICEF) and United Nations Office for Coordination of Humanitarian Affairs (UNOCHA) among others. He has travelled to different countries such as Kenya, Rwanda, South Africa, Somalia, Nigeria, Belgium, Spain, Netherlands and the United States. He is a member of International Leadership Association (ILA), The Christian Booksellers Association (CBA) and the Africa Strategic Leadership Forum (ASLF).

Dr. Odeke is also the Founder and Chairman of Centre for Transformation and Servant Leadership (CTSL Uganda). The organization's primary mission is to equip and empower aspiring leaders through resources, training and mentoring to serve humanity. Dr. Odeke is an author, speaker, teacher, trainer, educator, advisor, mentor, coach, consultant, leader, philanthropist and aid worker. He is also a leadership and management expert. He focuses on teaching success principles, overcoming crises, leadership, character, purpose, vision, potential and mentoring. Dr. Odeke believes that leadership can be developed through empowering, coaching, training and mentoring.

He is the author of the following works:

1. **Success Principles:** *Proven Secrets for Achieving Your Dreams and Vision.*

2. **Becoming an Influential Leader:** *How to Gain and Sustain it with Others in Your Generation.*

3. **Overcoming Crises:** *Strategies for Addressing, Managing and Recovering from Any Crisis.*

4. **Excellent Character:** *A Principal Requirement for Successful Leadership.*

5. **10 Principal Questions of Life:** *That Successful People Ask and Answer but People Who Fail Ignore and Neglect.*

6. **Strategic Planning:** *Understanding the 3Ps — The Power, Purpose and Process.*

7. **The Pillars for Sustaining Life:** *Discover What You Need to Live an Intentional Life.*

8. **Becoming a True Leader:** *Discovering Your Leadership Gift, Destiny and Purpose.*

9. **Overcoming Fear:** *How to Become in Charge of Your Life.*

10. **Life Game Plan:** *Strategies for Effectiveness in Your Second Half.*

11. **Life Flight Plan:** *A Sure Way to Arrive at Your Destination.*

12. **The Pursuit of a True Vision:** *Understanding The Secrets to Your Destiny in Life.*

REFERENCES

1. https://www.brainyquote.com/quotes/helen_keller_101301.

2. 1 Corinthians 12.

3. https://www.brainyquote.com/quotes/benjamin_disraeli_129996

4. https://due.com/blog/benjamin-franklin-growth-and-progress/

5. https://www.brainyquote.com/quotes/benjamin_franklin_151646

6. M.Scott Peck, *The Road Less Travelled* (New York: Touchstone, 1978), 15.

7. Ibid,15.

8. Joshua 1:7.

9. Proverbs 18:16.

10. Anonymous.

11. https://www.brainyquote.com/quotes/earl_nightingale_134690

12. https://www.brainyquote.com/quotes/oprah_winfrey_387162

13. https://www.brainyquote.com/lists/authors/top_10_viktor_e_frankl_quotes

14. Proverbs 23:7

15. Kent M. Keith, *The Silent Revolution: Dynamic Leadership in the Student Council*

16. 2 Corinthians 9:7.

17. Ibid

18. Mark 10: 45.

19. https://www.success.com/rohn-the-4-building-blocks-of-good-communication/

20. Mark11:22.

21. John 8:32.

22. John 14: 6.

23. Jeremiah 29:11.

24. Hebrew 11: 6.

25. Mark 11: 22.

26. Proverbs 22:6.

27. Philippians 3:12-14.

28. https://www.psychologytoday.com/us/blog/the-gift-maybe/201504/if-you-judge-people-you-have-no-time-love-them

29. https://scholarscompass.vcu.edu/cgi/viewcontent.cgi?article=1016&context=vcoa_editorial

30. Genesis 1: 28.

31. Proverbs 14:7.

32. https://www.goodreads.com/quotes/7067021-it-is-health-that-is-real-wealth-and-not-pieces.

33. https://mashable.com/2010/08/05/number-of-books-in-the-world/#x54rwcIFPmqH.

34. Ecclesiastes 1:9.

35. Claude M. Bristol, *The Magic of Believing* (New York: Pocket Books, 1994).

36. John 5:1-5.

37. https://vision.org.au/the-word-for-today/2017/09/16/become-a-good-thinker/

38. https://vision.org.au/the-word-for-today/2017/09/16/become-a-good-thinker/

39. Romans 12:2.

40. 1 Timothy 6:10.

41. Ecclesiastes 5:10.

42. https://www.azquotes.com/author/7129-Lee_Iacocca

43. https://www.brainyquote.com/authors/scott_caan

44. Philippians 3:13-14.

45. https://en.wikipedia.org/wiki/Pareto_principle

46. https://www.goodreads.com/author/quotes/16380.Carl_Sandburg

47. https://www.brainyquote.com/quotes/william_james_108497

48. Genesis 2:28.

49. https://www.forbes.com/quotes/5651/

50. Jim Collins, *Good to Great* (New York: Harper Business, 2001), 67.

51. Matthew 20: 25-28.

52. Matthew 22:39.

53. https://quoteinvestigator.com/2017/11/20/value/

54. Romans 10:9-10.

www.ingramcontent.com/pod-product-compliance
Lightning Source LLC
Chambersburg PA
CBHW072343090426
42741CB00012B/2895